To: Liz

Merry Christmas, 2009

~ Bunchie

1960 ATLANTA CRACKERS: SCOTT BREEDEN, SHELLY BRODSKY, LARRY BURRIGHT, DOUG CAMILLI, RICK CRONK, TIM HARKNESS, BOB "POOCHIE" HARTSFIELD, JIM HARWELL, JIM KORANDA, BILL LAJOIE, DON LeJOHN, RUBE WALKER - MANAGER, DICK SCOTT, ED STEVENS - COACH, CHARLIE SPELL, GENE SNYDER, JACK SMITH, DICK TRACEWSKI, PETE RICHERT, GENE WALLACE, JIM WILLIAMS

(PHOTOS ©2003 JEFFREY W. MOREY)

THE CRACKERS

THE CRA

CKERS

EARLY DAYS OF ATLANTA BASEBALL

TIM DARNELL

HILL STREET PRESS
ATHENS, GEORGIA

A
HILL
STREET
PRESS
BOOK
Published in the United
States of America by
Hill Street Press LLC
191 East Broad Street, Suite 209
Athens, Georgia 30601-2848 USA 706-613-7200
info@hillstreetpress.com • www.hillstreetpress.com
Hill Street Press books are available in bulk purchase and
customized editions to institutions and corporate accounts. Please
contact us for more information. • Our best efforts have been used to
obtain proper copyright clearance and credit for each of the images in this
book. If an unavoidable and inadvertent credit error has occurred it will be
corrected in future editions upon notification. Photographers hold copyrights to their
works. • No material in this book may be reproduced, scanned, stored, or transmitted in any
form, including all electronic and print media, or otherwise used without the prior written
consent of the publisher. However, an excerpt not to exceed 500 words may be used
one time only by newspaper and magazine editors solely in conjunction with a
review of or feature article about this book, the author, or Hill Street Press,
LLC. Attribution must be provided including the publisher's name,
author's name, and title of the book. • Copyright ©2003 by
Timothy Darnell. All rights reserved. Foreword copyright
©2003 by Bill Shipp. All rights reserved.
Afterword copyright ©2003 by Bobby Dews.
All rights reserved. Text design by Anne
Richmond Boston. Printed in the
United States of America.
Title page: Aerial view
of Ponce de Leon Ball
Park, circa
1962.

Library of Congress Cataloging-in-Publication Data

Darnell, Tim, 1961–
The Crackers : early days of Atlanta baseball / by Tim Darnell.
p.   cm.
Includes bibliographical references.
ISBN 1-58818-077-8 (alk. paper)
1. Atlanta Crackers (Baseball team) 2. Atlanta Black Crackers (Baseball team) I. Title.
GV875.A85 D37 2002
796.357'64'089960730758231—dc21   2001039444

ISBN # 1-58818-077-8
10 9 8 7 6 5 4 3 2 1
First printing

To Susan, for her tireless, loving patience
in putting up with my various endeavors.

Before we had the Braves, the Atlanta Crackers were our team, and it was truly an exciting adventure to ride to Atlanta, where my uncle would buy and sell mules. Then we would visit Sears, Roebuck & Co., and then go across the street to see our heroes play baseball. This made me the envy of our town.

—Jimmy Carter

CONTENTS

PREFACE

I first started paying serious attention to baseball right around the time that free agency began. A guy named Ted Turner signed this pitcher, Andy Messersmith, to play for his team and all of a sudden people were up in arms about how much money a ballplayer should make. I guess I was a little young to really understand what the big deal was about. All I knew was that my hometown team had a big-name thrower to go along with the only other pitcher who'd ever won anything for us, a knuckleballer named Niekro.

From that point on, though, I remember a lot of players who wore the Atlanta uniform, many of whom had been stars elsewhere and were expected to bring their winning ways to us.

Most of them didn't.

Still, there were highlights along the way: rookie Bob Horner blasting home runs out of Atlanta-Fulton County Stadium; Dale Murphy winning the National League MVP title not once but twice; and Gene Garber striking out—and thus ending—Pete Rose's pursuit of a Ty Cobb hitting record. Mostly, though, I remember a lot of losing.

Maybe that's what made '91 so thrilling. Finally, at long last, Atlanta was a winner. We would have been happy with just a division title, but to go to the World Series, of all things, was a feeling that couldn't be matched.

But Atlanta's success in baseball didn't begin with the '91 Braves. In fact, it didn't begin with the Braves at all. It began with teams that, until I started researching this book, I'd only known through local lore.

I don't remember those early days of Atlanta baseball, but I've talked to plenty of people who do. The memories of their experiences, so readily and willingly shared, have made this work possible.

This is mostly the story of the Atlanta Crackers, the old Southern Association's all-time winningest team. In a game mesmerized by statistics, the Atlanta Crackers won six league championships from 1895 to 1925.

Between 1925 and 1960 the Crackers won 11 pennants as well as six playoff titles; the 25 teams fielded by "Mr. Atlanta Baseball," Earl Mann, won 10 of those pennants. Only the New York Yankees won more pennants during the same period.

Likewise, for 59 years the Southern Association was baseball's finest, most stable organization, and led minor-league baseball into the height of its national popularity, right after World War II.

In any historical research, even that dealing with the not-so-distant past, one may find that record-keeping was sparse and sporadic. This is certainly the case in the history of early baseball and differences occasionally arise among researchers regarding won-loss statistics, personal bests and the like. In this book, I've used what I believe to be the most accurate and reliable sources of statistical information, those being Bill O'Neal's *The Southern League: Baseball in Dixie, 1885–1994; The Official Association Record Book* and *The Official International League Record Book.* While some published accounts may differ with these sources, my goal is to make this volume the definitive record of the Atlanta Crackers and the Black Crackers, and I have made what I believe to be the best decisions regarding the accuracy of the stats presented here.

When it came to providing the definitive photographic record of the Black Crackers, this researcher ran into a common problem. For reasons of racism, changes of team ownership and lack of proper archiving of photographs, there are not as many images of the BCs in this book as I would have liked. Despite a long and intense search, few printable images could be found. The best are, perhaps, waiting to be discovered in locked-away private collections.

Nonetheless, the best way to research baseball history is to talk with those who lived it. Players, managers, sportswriters and fans still here to enjoy their twilight years spent many afternoons regaling me with tales of players riding in "cattle cars," afternoon doubleheaders in flannel uniforms, and fans who wore their Sunday best when spending the day at the park. They've allowed me to visit a time when baseball was played for the sheer enjoyment that only this game can offer.

The Crackers: Early Days of Atlanta Baseball has been written for those who remember the team and the old Southern Association, the many players and owners who formed the best-run and most well-organized minor-league operation the sport had ever seen.

And this history has been written in the hope that youngsters will read about the players, owners and devoted fans who participated in and witnessed our national pastime the way it was meant to be enjoyed.

The way it still *should* be.

FOREWORD

It must have been in the mid-1940s. The war was still going on. I can't remember the exact date, but it was a Saturday. It was the day I knew I was accepted as a man. My dad let me go to Atlanta with him—and let me sit in the outfield bleachers at Poncey to watch the Atlanta Crackers play the Birmingham Barons.

Oh, I'd been to baseball games before. I never missed watching the Bell Bombers in Marietta. But it was a semi-pro club—or was it strictly amateur? I don't recall. In any event, the Bombers played in little ball yards—and mostly for amusement.

But seeing the Crackers play the Barons at Ponce de Leon Park Ball Park? As far as I was concerned, that was as good as was watching the Cardinals play the stinking Dodgers. Maybe watching the Crackers wasn't quite big-league baseball, but it was big-time baseball.

Watching the actual game, however, was not the main part of the rite of passage. It was sitting in the bleachers with the gruff, whiskey-swigging men. That's when I knew my dad thought I was finally ready to come into the club of Southern Sportsmen, as an associate underage member, of course. The Sportsmen, mostly in their forties, sat in shirtsleeves, laughing and shouting at one another—and pulling wads of dollar bills from their pockets and passing the bucks around. They were betting, mostly on outfield flies. A dollar could win you five—if the hitter flew to the outfield. A few guys who were really into it also gambled on strikes and balls and even fouls. A couple of sweaty fat guys with huge stacks of bills booked the bets. Every few minutes, my dad or one of the men would pull a pint flask from his pocket and take a long swig, followed by a wince at the terrible taste of the stuff. The action—and the talk—was so fast that I couldn't keep up with it.

At one point during the game, a couple of Atlanta cops came around. Amazingly, the gambling ceased as if it had never occurred. The bottles likewise disappeared. The two bookies became intensely interested in what was happening on the field, as they debated the merits of various infielders. The outfield bleachers suddenly seemed filled with a group of country deacons who had come to Atlanta to enjoy an afternoon's outing at Ponce de Leon Ball Park.

As soon as the cops disappeared, the money and liquor reappeared. The jokes started again. The shouting and betting started up as if they had never stopped.

It was one of the truly fun days of my life. The best part of it, though, was that I had bragging rights with my buddies for weeks afterward. I told them about the whole episode and embellished it to make the great "Tiny Shipp," as I was then called, appear to be a central figure in the drama of the bleachers.

When I drive on Ponce de Leon Avenue today, past the old Sears building, and look toward the overdeveloped site of long-gone Poncey, I can almost hear the sounds and smell the smells of that Saturday afternoon, when I felt for the first time just like one of the men.

By the way, when I was born, my Aunt Edna, who was from Alabama, insisted that my mom and dad name me Baron in honor of her favorite team. My folks said that just wouldn't be right because we lived so close to Poncey, home of the great Atlanta Crackers.

Too bad. "Baron Shipp" would have been a helluva by-line.

BILL SHIPP

POPCORN!
PEANUTS!

BATTING PRACTICE

WHERE CENTER FIELD IS FOREVER

"Baseball is a reflection of the American viewpoint respecting every important question. This viewpoint is expressed by the nature of the game upon the playing field and is expressed by the administrative structure that governs the organization of professional baseball. Baseball is American democracy in action."

—Eddie Glennon, Atlanta Crackers General Manager, 1965

S hielded from the sun, the small mound of dirt that used to be focal point for the hottest seat in town was now covered by a large tent. Instead of a flannel-uniformed ballplayer, a man in the '60s uniform of business—a grey flannel suit—stood atop the mound which, despite the ever-so-fast-changing times, still was the center of everyone's attention.

On this occasion, however, the only people in the grand old stadium were a few hundred real estate men, bankers and lawyers. The only link to the glory of bygone days was provided by the presence of "Mr. Atlanta Baseball" himself.

"Progress must continue," said Earl Mann on October 25, 1965. "We now have a magnificent new stadium for both baseball and football. That means old Poncey has to go. Part of my dream—having Major League Baseball for this city I love—has come true, and that's a comforting thought."

But the day she fell, the local baseball faithful said that a curse was placed on whatever or whoever would move onto this sacrosanct piece of earth. And, sure enough, dozens of establishments have come and gone through the years, most plagued by the dreaded consumer whammy of apathy.

Ponce de Leon Ball Park—or old Poncey, as many called her. For 58 years, one of the winningest teams in baseball history called her home; only Yankee Stadium housed more championship winners in organized baseball than Poncey did over that same period of time.

As part of a circuit populated by fields with eccentric personalities, tricky short hops and never-before-seen sight lines, the ballpark was the crown jewel of the old Southern Association. She had her quirks, plenty of them, in fact—a kudzu-covered hill and a giant magnolia, both in fair territory, being the most memorable. Babe Ruth once bounced a double into the tree and Eddie Mathews hit a few into its branches. One player (who, despite being named Jack Daniels, was not a descendent of the legendary whiskey distiller) spent more time in the kudzu chasing down fly balls than he did between the white lines. And a certain tall, skinny farm boy from northwest Georgia, Ralph "Country" Brown, knew how to use that tree and bank to his advantage, so much so that some people even named the hill after him for awhile.

The Atlantans, though, the ones who turned out in droves to cheer their heroes named Montag, Tanner, and hundreds of others, did as much to make Poncey the South's premier ballpark as the players did. Other than Grant Field at Georgia Tech, this field was the only game in town. Box seats at Poncey were once as prized as luxury suites currently are at Turner Field.

During the decades when the minor leagues were the major leagues to Atlanta, Poncey was jam-packed with fans of all kinds, sizes and shapes. Most of all, there were kids, and lots of them. Over the decades, hundreds of thousands of them rushed through Poncey's turnstiles with their dads. While their household's civilized bread-winner called upon the wrath of the Lord to descend upon the umpires, children covered with ketchup, Coke and ice-cream stains romped up and down the stairwells.

Atlanta was known as a good baseball town, mostly because it led the league in attendance over every other city in the South. Naturally, every now and then, a New Orleans, Little Rock or Birmingham would hit a homer with a magnificent year at the box office, but the name at the top of the attendance roll call usually was *Atlanta*.

Along with everything else in the South, Poncey was segregated. But her largest crowd ever turned out to see a single black man play baseball. It happened during a 1949 three-game exhibition series when Jackie Robinson and the Brooklyn Dodgers visited Poncey and her home team, marking the first time in Atlanta history that blacks and whites competed against each other in a professional sporting event of any kind, at any level. The final game drew the all-time Poncey record of 25,221, including 13,885 black fans.

Then, in the 1950s, it all began to change.

Minor-league baseball stopped being the public enterprise that the civic-minded populace thought was their obligation to support with their attendance. Television brought baseball into our dens and living rooms, and a newly air-conditioned American dream with a fuzzy black-and-white tube became preferable to a stifling, sticky, living-color afternoon at the park.

3

People slowly stopped coming to Poncey and other Southern Association parks, and the league, once the game's best, died in 1961. Poncey's home team hung around for a few years after that, as a Triple-A club in the International League, one that actually won a couple of titles themselves. But the team never captured the city's imagination as they had in the old days.

Then the Braves came.

For the first time in American sports history, a major-league franchise was going to set up shop south of the Mason-Dixon Line. "I can almost hear the sound of the bat cracking against the ball," Mayor Ivan Allen, Jr., said, as he announced the i's had been dotted and the t's crossed on the contract that would bring the Braves to Dixie.

But away from all of the hubbub and commotion, Ponce de Leon Ball Park, once a symbol of triumph and civic pride, turned into a forgotten relic of the musty, cobweb-ridden past. And hardly a soul grimaced as she turned from a lushly green diamond into a beercan-strewn trash heap. She was carved up, slice by slice, even before the wrecking ball began falling on the historic black neighborhoods that had to be cleared away before Atlanta Stadium arose. Poncey's batting cage and a few of her seats would wind up at a local university, other parts Lord-knows-where.

The auction was handled by J.L. Todd Auction. Colonel Pierce Smith handled the affair, keeping up his auctioneer's chant for almost five consecutive hours. But before he began, he asked organist Dale Stone to play "Take Me Out to the Ball Game," because "Earl Mann says he wants to hear it one more time here in the ballpark."

"I hate to see it go; a little bit of me goes with it," Mann said that day. "There are a lot of memories out there, and I do face this day with mixed emotions. Old Poncey's had its day, but that it has to go is something that must be accepted. It had no future as we knew it in the past.

It was the greatest with its intimacy, but minor-league ball is running out of angels.

"There isn't anybody to put up the money any more. The majors own it all now, and they'll have to pay the freight and run it all now. It's great that the Braves will be here now, and I'm very proud of any part I might have had in their coming.

"Old Man Fate and baseball have been pretty good to me."

By 3:00 P.M., Poncey was no more.

"We've got to study what can be developed here. It's a wonderful piece of property and I think the price was fair, for both buyer and seller. We believe in the growth of Atlanta and think that this property will be a most important part of that growth." So said Clarence Howard, a representative of Allan Grayson Realty, which bought the

Atlanta's field of dreams, Ponce de Leon Ball Park, pictured before 1949 when a 2-foot hedge was planted from left field to center field to reduce home-run distances.

park's land and an adjacent estate, 23 acres, for $1,250,000, on behalf of "unnamed parties."

For decades after the auction, sparse strips of grass and bush among vast expanses of white-lined asphalt were all that was left of her playing field. Rotting weeds covered the embankment along her right-field line that used to be lushly green with grass. And the train tracks that once carried a home-run ball more than 500 miles were rusting away.

Today, however, as young, upwardly mobile ex-suburbanites, wearied by too many excruciating hours behind the wheel, move back into Atlanta's city limits, a massive example of that new breed of commercial development called urban mixed-use sits on old Poncey's grounds. You can find a home improvement warehouse, a trendy bookstore and one of those ever-popular specialty coffee shops on her infields and beyond. Maybe Earl Mann's vision for the property that he expressed on the day of the auction has finally come true: "I'd like to see something to benefit the city of Atlanta, and I'm sure whatever is built will be good for the city."

Still standing, however, out there where center field is forever, is the giant magnolia, a silent sentinel that has witnessed the transformation of two dozen acres from symbol of civic pride to urban flotsam and now back again to something that is shiny and new, an icon of the past that now greets shoppers rather than sluggers.

PLAY BALL!!

FIRST INNING

SOUTHERN CRUMBS TO ATLANTA CRACKERS

"I'm going to have baseball news . . ."

Henry W. Grady

T hick carpets of green grass still glistening from the summer dew greeted the crowds of people who started arriving shortly after the breakfast hour. Most came on foot, excitedly gathering around the field as the sun rose higher in the sky, while those remaining few still preoccupied with social appearances came in gaily decorated carriages, adorned with ribbons, buntings and streamers that fluttered in the light, cool breezes.

The morning, though dawned bright and clear, held the promise of thick waves of sweltering, suffocating afternoon heat. So the drivers of the horse-drawn wagonettes, almost by instinct alone, headed for the shade offered by the stout young oaks surrounding the field.

Cleared for only a few short weeks, the grounds held a natural diamond near a town cemetery where, only a few days before, fresh summer flowers had been laid at the feet of the Confederate dead in a tender gesture of annual remembrance.

But today . . . well, today would be different. Today would host a far more happy occasion, because today the finest team on the planet would meet an upstart group of young men who'd dared to challenge their supremacy in the game of baseball.

Such was the scene on May 12, 1866, Atlanta's first-ever game of professional, organized baseball. Probably no single sporting event in the city has ever been looked upon with more of a sense of diversion and relief since that early summer afternoon. Atlanta was still partially in ruin from the fires of William T. Sherman and federal troops still occupied every nook and cranny of the city. Among the population of about 20,000, several hundred cases of smallpox had been reported. Bright red flags hung from the doors of those houses afflicted with the nightmarish disease.

The sick and the poor were everywhere. So desperate were the mayor and town council for money that they appealed to Midwestern cities for credit to feed those starving people on relief. Lawlessness had broken out in every section of town, with burglaries and other crimes commonplace.

Several decades before, the game of baseball had been introduced. Since the 1840s, when the New York Knickerbockers and 15 other baseball clubs had joined together to form the National Association of Base Ball Players, the game had been capturing the public's imagination all over the nation. During the long years of the war, Union and Confederate soldiers alike had learned the primitive game and were now bringing it home with them. Now, in the midst of poverty and pessimism, Tom Burnett, who ran an ice house on Atlanta's Wall Street (now part of Underground Atlanta) decided to organize a local team, the Atlanta Baseball Club, and the sporting craze began to spread throughout the city faster than Sherman's flames ever had.

A field was cleared on Hunter Street next to Oakland Cemetery, and once Burnett picked his team, entire families and friends gathered there three afternoons each week to watch their husbands, fathers, neighbors and boyfriends "swing the willow stick," blister their white hands catching the ball, and exhaust themselves running the bases.

The players were as green as the grass they played on. But these were the young beaux of the town, many of whom had returned only scarcely a year before from the fighting front. The game provided an escape from the horror of the war and its aftermath, only less than two years after all but about 400 of Atlanta's homes and businesses had been reduced to ashes.

THE FINEST TEAM ON THE PLANET

After only a few weeks of practice, Burnett proclaimed himself captain of the "finest team in the world," ready to meet all challengers. They didn't have to wait very long. An Atlantan named Robert Dohme then organized the Gate City Nine, and once his team of young players came together, their sole purpose in life was to beat the living tar out of Burnett and his boys.

By game day, a full-scale fashion war had broken out, with each club trying to outdress the other. First marching onto the field was Burnett's Atlanta Baseball Club. Dressed in black broadcloth trousers with wide glazed leather belts, white flannel shirts and white caps, his team featured "Coach" Alexander, Edgar Thompson, Joe Ormond, Robert Soloman, Sonny Wright, Tiff Meade, Joe Bridges and Hayne Ellis.

Then out paraded the Gate City Nine, proudly attired in knee-length light blue trousers with a red stripe down the

9

sides, orange shirts and shiny black military-style caps. Dohme, besides serving as captain, played shortstop; John Collier was at first base; Willis Biggers at second; Tom Johnson, third; Bill Judson, left field; Dick Williford played center; Bill Sparks was in right; George Cassin played behind—way behind—the plate; and James Gregg pitched for the Gate City Nine.

Chairs for the players were set up along both sides of the diamond. Atlanta's very first umpire, a local saloon owner named Samuel T. Downs, sat in a huge armchair near home plate. At precisely 2:00 P.M., the teams marched onto the diamond to the music of a brass band. From his great armchair, Downs bellowed, "Play ball!"

And play they did, on and on, into the twilight, to the delight of the audience. There was no admission fee, no grandstands, no peanuts, popcorn or cold drinks. The fans had simply come to enjoy the entertainment, freed, if only for a moment, from the daily struggle to survive with just a piece of their charred dignity.

Several accidents occurred during the game, not the least of which was a ball that struck Dohme in the stomach. Some of the women and children fainted or cried at the horrifying sight, as the captain's recruits struggled to revive him. After a short break in the action, Dohme recovered enough to stay in the contest.

The balls were not thrown with any sort of windup; there were no curves or fastballs. They were tossed out with careless grace, so it isn't surprising that at least 25 runs were scored in the first inning. The game was stopped only long enough for the players to rest themselves between innings, when needed. No gloves or masks were worn.

Few rules were on the books to guide the players, and spectators had a hard time dodging the balls that came flying in their direction. One of the Gate City Nine was reported to hit a ball so far that it wasn't located until two weeks later, a quarter of a mile away from the field.

Finally, at 6:30 P.M., the last man in the last inning was declared out. The Gate City Nine had accomplished their then-lifelong mission, whipping the Atlanta Baseball Club—by a final score of 127–29. So proud were the players of their victory they gilded the ball they had used and

Nicknames for Atlanta's Historic Baseball Teams	
Atlantas	(1885–86, 1889, 1894)
Firecrackers	(1892)
Windjammers	(1893)
Crackers	(1896–97, 1902–1965)

engraved it with the club name and the date. Then they put it on display at a popular downtown pharmacy, Taylor's Drug Store, so everyone could look at it in passing.

Though Burnett's club disbanded, the Gate City Nine lived on to play against the other teams which had begun springing up over the state. During the rest of the summer, they won 36 games, playing Georgia teams from Augusta, Columbus, Macon, Rome, as well as clubs from Charleston, S.C., and Montgomery, Ala. They played many of their home games in City Park, between the Union Depot and Alabama Street, now also part of Underground Atlanta and the Cola-Cola Museum. Their only loss of the season came from a group of Athens college students who called themselves the Dixie Club.

The final game of Atlanta's first organized baseball season was in Knoxville, Tenn., on July 4, 1866. The hometown Holstons, so sure were they of their own victory, had planned a banquet after the game. But after losing to Gate City 21–19, they were so enraged that they called off the entire event and refused to speak to the Atlanta players, leaving the Gate City Nine alone to enjoy a huge cake made by one of Knoxville's most eligible young ladies, Miss Laura Baxter.

After every game of that season, the Gate City Nine gilded and inscribed a baseball recording their victory. No record exists of the fate of these 36 priceless mementos.

But soon other loosely organized teams began sprouting

11

up throughout the state, as baseball took the state—and the South—by storm.

Smith Clayton, in addition to being a member of the Gate City Nine and later a player for an Athens, Ga., team, was a contributor to the *Atlanta Herald* and *City Builder*. He wrote that "people gazed in mute astonishment at these wonderful players, would yell themselves hoarse when by accident the catcher would take a foul on the bounce, and would become crazy with delight when some nervous fielder would grab up the ball, as if he were digging turnips."

HENRY W. GRADY, NO. 1 BASEBALL FAN

By the late 1860s and early 1870s, Atlanta was well on its way to recovery from the devastation of the Civil War. The city was made capitol of Georgia in 1868, the same year the *Atlanta Constitution* was founded. Two years later, the city's first trolley service began operating.

The next major organized team to appear in Atlanta were the Osceolas in 1872, only three short years after the game's first avowedly professional team, the Cincinnati Red Stockings, had organized, and only one year after the National Association of Professional Base Ball Players was formed. The Osceolas' star players were "the South's invincible pitcher, Ed Payne," and Charles Pemberton, son of John S. Pemberton, the inventor of the Coca-Cola formula.

After one undefeated season they met their Waterloo in Rome, Ga., when they faced a team fielded by Henry W. Grady, then with the *Rome Tribune* and already solidifying his reputation as one of the South's premier journalists. There being no rule preventing outsiders from playing, Grady slipped in a pitcher from New York and the Osceolas were shut out, with one hit and no runs. The players were so disgusted they quit the team, thus ending the brief saga of the Osceolas.

The Atlanta Tullers, named for the Deep South's long genealogical ties to the Scottish highlanders who had migrated to the region, were organized in 1876 (the same year when the National Association of Professional Base Ball Players became the National Association of Professional Base Ball Clubs, a group of owners who would dominate the game at the national level for the next quarter century and who also created the reserve clause, which would become the most significant labor issue in professional sports history). Ed and Bart Baldwin, Lem Butler, Lewis Morrison, Charles Pemberton, John Savage, Bill Maddox, Alf Cassin and Charlie Read were all stars of the Atlanta team. They organized to play a Macon, Ga.-based club who claimed to be champions of the 1876 season, whatever that was. Over a series of games in both cities, the Tullers bested the Maconites.

By October 1881, the 31-year-old Grady had moved on to become managing editor of the *Atlanta Constitution,* and his insatiable interest in the game had grown even stronger than it was during his days in Rome. The paper was spending more money than any other publication in the South on telegraph wire news services, so Grady could include game results and box scores in the *Constitution.*

Editor-in-chief Evan P. Howell was so worried about the growing expenses that he told Grady to stop using the services "or I'm going to charge [costs] to you!" Grady, undaunted, replied, "Charge it. I don't care. But I'm going to have baseball news just the same."

In 1884 baseball fever had reached such a pitch that this announcement appeared in the *Constitution* in July: "A movement is on foot to organize a Southern baseball league which will admit one or more clubs from each city that has over 75,000 inhabitants. It is understood that Atlanta, Nashville, Memphis, Little Rock and other city clubs have signified their willingness to enter such an association. Efforts are being made to bring about a favorable result and

13

soon a meeting of leading baseball men will be called. With such an organization the South could give encouragement to this leading and popular field sport."

THE SOUTH'S FIRST BASEBALL LEAGUE

Thus it was on November 23, 1884, in Montgomery, Ala., that the South's first professional baseball organization was born. Grady was elected president of the Southern League, and its first official playing season would be 1885.

The original league consisted of Atlanta (Atlantas), Augusta (Browns), Columbus (Stars) and Macon, Ga.; Birmingham, Ala.; and Chattanooga (Lookouts), Memphis (Browns) and Nashville (Americans), Tenn. At one time or another from 1885–1896 teams were fielded in Charleston, S.C.; Charlotte, N.C.; Montgomery and Mobile, Ala.; New Orleans and Savannah, Ga.

The Southern League was professional baseball's first minor league to launch a 100-game schedule, although Birmingham (17–64) didn't complete the season, the Columbus Stars (42–39) played just 81 games and the Chattanooga Lookouts (30–59) played 89. The Atlanta Atlantas, the Nashville Americans, and the Memphis Browns did play more than 90 games each, while the Augusta Browns and Macon played 104 and 106 games respectively.

Grady took his duties as league president very seriously, so much so that several teams threatened to withdraw before the inaugural season was over. He was strict in his demands that players refrain from associating with "questionable characters" and he was determined to keep rowdy behavior at the games to a minimum. He wanted nothing to prevent baseball from becoming a wholesome, family-oriented entertainment medium, which would make the game all the more profitable.

14

A WINNING TRADITION BEGINS

Atlanta, with a record of 60–31, narrowly edged Augusta (68–36) for the first Southern League pennant in 1885, thus setting in motion a championship trend in organized, professional baseball that would last over the next 80 years. Leading the Atlantas were outfielder Walt Goldsby (.305 with 89 runs scored), shortstop John Cahill (.295 with 90 runs in 90 games) and catcher-outfielder George McVey (.290). All three would eventually play in the major leagues and every position player except the center fielder (who hit a measly .177) and first baseman (a poor .210) were past or future big leaguers.

In fact, most of the top Southern League players would see action in the bigs, and fans came to expect only the finest around the circuit's wooden ballparks. Salaries ranged between $50 and $60 per month, though top players in the league sometimes earned $75 a month.

Although Birmingham and Columbus didn't return in 1886, the Southern League finished its second season with Atlanta blazing another trail to the league title (the same year that Jacob's Pharmacy began selling Coca-Cola). With a season-ending record of 64–28 (.695), the team was led by future big leaguers John Cline (who won the batting title with an average of .353 and 56 stolen bases), third baseman Dennis Lyons (.316), stolen-base leader Blondy Purcell (.267 with 72 stolen bases and the best fielding percentage among league left fielders), and pitchers John Schafer and Richard Conway, who won 22 and 20 games respectively.

A COMPLETELY DIFFERENT GAME

Southern League-brand baseball of the 19th century resembled our fast-pitch softball of today. The pitching distance was 50 feet; pitches were thrown underhanded. The bases were 90 feet apart, but first and third were outside the foul lines (they

15

were moved inside the playing field in 1886.) Fielders' gloves were small and thin; catchers wore no protective equipment and positioned themselves far behind the batters. Seven balls had to be taken for a batter to be awarded first base.

The game of the 19th century was rough, and probably no one had it rougher than the umpire—umpire, as in, singular. He called the game from 40 feet behind home plate; when men were on base, he moved behind the pitcher. Usually only one official worked a game, and he was the target of curses, flying objects and physical attacks. Indeed, sometimes the game's most prominent officials encouraged assaulting the umpire. A.G. Spalding of the Chicago White Stockings saw nothing wrong with it; he said it was fans' democratic right as Americans to oppose tyranny in any form.

The Atlantas played at Peters Park at the corner of North Avenue and West Peachtree, where BellSouth now calls home. The park (named after Richard Peters, a devout baseball fan who donated to the construction of North Avenue so fans would have easy access to the games) also was near an Atlanta Street Railway trolley line. Wooden grandstands and bleachers were enclosed by a tall wire fence.

Despite the baseball craze, however, the Southern League suffered from a tremendous amount of franchise switching and financial instability. In 1887, Atlanta dropped out of the league, leaving Grady's original Southern League to fold in 1888 after only four cities—Birmingham, Charleston, Memphis and New Orleans—fielded teams.

In the spring of 1889, a newly reorganized Southern League was born, launched by Atlanta, Chattanooga, Mobile and New Orleans; they were later joined by Birmingham, Charleston and Memphis. But Atlanta, burdened by financial problems and a losing record on top of that, dropped out early in the season, followed by Memphis and

The 1886 Atlanta Base Ball Club.
National Baseball Hall of Fame Library

Birmingham. This "Great Minor League Failure of 1889" was the third straight early collapse of the Southern League, and it couldn't be restored in 1890 or 1891.

By 1892, however, baseball fans and city leaders in eight Southern towns, including Atlanta, once again revived professional, organized competition. The city's population had grown to more than 65,000; the Equitable Building, Atlanta's first skyscraper, had opened, and Asa Candler founded the Coca-Cola Co.

17

The Atlanta Firecrackers finished at 58–65 for the season, which also marked the first time in the history of the league that every team played 120 or more games, the longest schedule of any Southern League to that date.

The Atlanta Windjammers were born in 1893, and they played a 12-team schedule plagued by travel problems, owners who sold off their star players to the majors (thus angering fans at the Southern box offices), and a vast disparity between first-place and 12th-place teams. Legend has it that the league schedule had been drawn up by a young lady friend of one of the owners. She had never seen a game of baseball, and the result was a very bulky, unworkable calendar. The intricate process of schedule creation was very unscientific in the 19th century.

South Atlanta's Brisbane Park, at Cumley, Glenn and Ira streets next the Atlanta Traction Co. rail line, hosted the Windjammers' home games. The company offered inducements to the team to move near its line, including the creation of a new transit route built to facilitate arriving and leaving the ballpark.

The 1893 season was also notable for the number of teams turned over to the league by their owners, including Birmingham, Nashville and Chattanooga. The league president resigned on July 1 and the '93 season was subsequently ended prematurely on August 12.

The 1894 season proved a little more stable, and baseball owners and players were optimistic for 1895. Six veteran cities sponsored clubs, including Atlanta, and new entries from Little Rock and Evansville, Ind., rounded out the eight-team circuit.

Old Southern League Ballparks	Atlanta		
	Peters Park: Built in 1885 at North Avenue and West Peachtree Street.	*Brisbane Park:* Located in south Atlanta at Cumley, Glenn and Ira streets. It was used for league play in 1892, 1985 and 1896.	*Athletic Grounds:* Consolidated Railway built this field adjacent to their tracks for the 1894 and 1895 seasons.

The Atlantas were owned and operated by prominent local politicians and controlled by a joint stock company. Joseph Hirsch, a local alderman and wealthy clothing merchant, was team president.

By 1895, the Atlantas had moved to the Athletic Grounds, built by the Consolidated Railway Co., which was the second-largest ballpark in the South. It was built on the old Shaw Ground, a large vacant field owned by a rich banker named Coker, who for years had rented out the grounds to circuses and fairs.

A DISAGREEABLE CHARACTER

Once the team settled in their new home, however, several prominent locals began protesting the "disagreeable character" of the baseball crowds. According to one account "noise from the park disturbed the residential community, and . . . order could not be maintained." Hirsch tried to use his political influence but failed. Despite his promise of an increased police presence during games, and even with Atlanta tied for first place, the city council suspended the team's license, an action followed by a howl of protest never before seen in baseball matters.

Local newspaper editorials called the clubs' owners "fine gentlemen" and argued that baseball was the summer's best entertainment, attracting more than half of the population. The *Atlanta Constitution* said that "Possum Trot and all other provincial villages of the country will point the finger of ridicule at us" if the baseball team were forced to shut down. Eventually the council relented, a compromise was reached for a trial period, and the team continued the season.

Birmingham

The Slag Pile: Built in the 1880s at 14th Street and First Avenue North. The grandstand could seat 600 fans, but beyond the outfield fence sat the slag pile of Alice Furnace, where many spectators would sit.

Chattanooga

Stanton Field: Built in the 1880s where the Stivers Lumber Co. would later sit.

19

◇

The 1895 pennant race was the hottest and closest battle in Southern baseball history to that point, and tempers flared throughout the league. At one point, Evansville was in second place and Atlanta held the third spot. A report from the *Atlanta Constitution* on July 14, 1895, stated that "the Atlantas went down before the (Evansville) Hoosiers for the second time yesterday by a score of 9–4. . . .

"After the game a gang of hoodlums followed the team and hooted and jeered and threw rocks at the Atlantas. [One player] was hit by a brick and received a painful scalp wound. True, the Atlantas were defeated and accepted their defeat like gentlemen, but such conduct as this is intolerable and the guilty parties ought to be punished."

On June 15, 1895, the Nashville Scraphs came to town. "Probably no game which has ever been played in Atlanta creates so much excitement as the one to take place today with Nashville," said the *Constitution*. "The bitter feeling which the *Nashville American* [newspaper] has created between the two cities has been heightened by the fact the Nashville club is now in second place, and by the knowledge that the ultimate struggle for the pennant will, in all probability, be between Atlanta and Nashville.

"The interest in these games is not confined to Atlanta alone, but at least 1,200 people from other cities will come to this city to witness the struggle. The Nashvilles arrived yesterday evening at the Kimball House. They are a fine looking body of men and A-1 ballplayers. They are in no way responsible for the unwarranted attacks which the Nashville press has made on the Atlanta club, and it is hoped they will

Old Southern League Ballparks

Dallas

Gaston Park: Built in the 1890s on the Texas State Fair Grounds.

Macon

Mulberry Park: The oldest grounds in town were at the end of Mulberry Street. By the time the city joined the Southern League, the grandstand was covered and a plank fence surrounded the park.

Daisy Park: Originally called Central City Park. The diamond was on the site of an old hippodrome, which was cut in half for use as a semicircular grandstand.

be treated in the same impartial manner by the audiences in which all other visiting clubs have been treated."

Atlanta posted the best season record of 1895, but Nashville protested a number of games, and when the league governors upheld their objections, Nashville claimed a controversial championship.

BIRTH OF THE CRACKERS

Why Atlanta chose the nickname "Crackers" for a baseball team is a matter of speculation. It was once a derogatory term for a poor white Southerner, but it's also been used to denote someone who is quick and efficient at any task. Another theory is that the team was named after the local plowboys who were good at cracking the whip over oxen and horses down on the farm. And it could just be a shortened version of the city's 1892 team, the Firecrackers.

In any event, the Atlanta Crackers were born in 1896, playing in Brisbane Park. Only six teams opened the season, though, and by June the 36–36 Atlanta Crackers and the 26–41 Birmingham Bluebirds had dropped out. Columbus, Mobile, Montgomery and New Orleans held on for another month, but never made the 100-game mark. Not a very auspicious beginning for a franchise destined to become the South's winningest minor-league baseball team.

The Southern League didn't reorganize in 1897. W.T. Moyers, a prominent local attorney, attempted to field a team from Atlanta in a new, makeshift alliance called the Southeastern League, but the club disbanded two months into the season. In early 1898, Moyers again tried

Memphis	Nashville	New Orleans
Olympic Park: The later site of the Memphis Area Transit Authority Bus Terminal. Olympic Park was built in the 1880s.	*Athletic Park:* Built at the Sulfur Spring Bottom where baseball had been played in the city since the 1860s.	*Crescent City Base Ball Park:* Built in 1880 and later renovated and enlarged to seat 5,000 fans in 1887. Later known as Sportsman's Park and Athletic Park.

21

to field an Atlanta club, arguing the city's transit companies shouldn't reap the financial benefits of a team without contributing to its upkeep.

Indeed, streetcar companies made big money from fares to ballparks in the early years of Southern baseball. Transit companies often owned the teams themselves just to keep this major entertainment attraction along their routes. Two separate transit companies operated in Montgomery, Ala., and each one had a ballfield at the end of their routes.

Moyers eventually convinced the Atlanta Street Railway Co. to back the team. On February 16, 1898, the reborn Atlanta Crackers joined the Southern League, with Moyers as president; F.M. Zimmerman, the railway's superintendent, as vice president; and Frank Sheridan as manager on a no-pennant/no-pay contract. But while the team played good ball, it withdrew from competition on May 20. Atlanta's owners were irate at the Birmingham Bluebirds and the New Orleans Pelicans, the association's only teams to refuse to contribute to league operating funds. Plus, the railway's projected profits of $3,000 a year never came, and it left hard feelings between the team and the railway company. A local city league was formed to finish out the 1898 Cracker season.

The original Southern League then breathed its last gasp in 1899, at the same time that the brand new American League was drawing the nation's top baseball talent from the National League. Yet despite failed franchises, abbreviated seasons and no play at all in 1891, 1892, 1897 and 1900, the Southern League had created an insatiable appetite for baseball in the South.

THE FINEST MINORS IN THE LAND

On October 20, 1900, in Birmingham, the Southern Association was born, destined to become the finest, most successful minor-league baseball operation in history. Atlanta was offered a spot—at no charge—in the new league, but no one could be found to provide any financial backing for the team itself.

Then Charles Abner Powell, a baseball pioneer and one of the most colorful characters in the annals of the game, entered the picture.

Ab Powell, a pitcher, catcher, infielder and outfielder all in one package, played two years in the majors, with Washington in the Union Association in 1884 and the American Association's Baltimore and Cincinnati teams in 1886. He went to New Orleans in 1887, and quickly made his considerable, charismatic presence felt.

As owner/manager of the expansion New Orleans Pelicans, Powell led his team to the league title in their inaugural season. Because of the frequent rains in the Crescent City, he devised both the idea of covering the infield with a tarpaulin during downpours and a system whereby fans with tickets to rained-out games kept their stub for readmittance to a later contest—the rain check.

Also in 1887, Powell convinced other club owners that on a certain day of the week, women should be admitted into the park free or at half-price. The first Ladies' Day was staged April 29, 1887, at Sportsman's Park in New Orleans, and soon Ladies' Day became a featured event at all Southern League ballparks. Eventually the majors adopted the idea as well.

Besides boosting the game's fan appeal, Ladies' Day became an important factor in helping to clean up the language used around the ballparks, both on the field and in the grandstands.

Along with Newt Fisher of Nashville and Charley Frank of Memphis, Powell was one of the organizers of the new Southern Association in 1900. When no one stepped forward to support an Atlanta team, Powell and partner E. T. Peters located their new team, the Christians, in Selma, Ala. This franchise, along with the Nashville Vols, Little Rock Travelers, Memphis

23

Egyptians, New Orleans Pelicans, Shreveport Tigers, Chattanooga Lookouts and Birmingham Barons, comprised the inaugural circuit. A salary cap of $1,200 a month for no more than 12 players was set.

A NEW FLOCK OF PELICANS

Selma was a debacle. The team lost money and plenty of games. To make matters worse for Powell, his New Orleans team was firmly entrenched in the cellar early in the year.

So when a road trip took Powell and his New Orleans team to Memphis, the resourceful owner armed himself with $1,200 and ventured into the North Carolina League to recruit an entirely new roster of Pelicans. He brought his new team back to Memphis, fired everyone on his old one and fielded the new players the very next day, unprecedented in baseball history.

The fired players sat in the stands that game and booed the rookies, but the new lineup beat the Egyptians in 11 innings, won 18 games in a row at one point and finished with a winning 68–55 record.

In 1901, Powell decided to move his Selma team (which had finished dead-last at 37–78) to Atlanta. Powell purchased a half-interest in the club for $2,000 and left New Orleans. In their first season in the Southern Association, the new Atlanta Crackers, with Powell as manager, finished fourth, winning 58 games and losing 60.

The following year, despite a 62–60 record, they again finished fourth, while the Nashville Vols, led by pitcher/outfielder Hugh Hill, won a second consecutive pennant. Hill led the league and set the all-time Southern Association batting average of .416 during that season.

By now, the original National Association classification system had taken effect, which organized the minor leagues by the size of their cities. There were Class A, B, C and D leagues, with the largest towns in A and the smallest in D. The Southern Association was designated as one of four B leagues. In 1905 it was elevated to Class-A status, with the American Association, Pacific Coast League, Eastern (later the International) League and Western League. By 1908 a Class-AA level was created, and the Southern Association and Western League were left as the only two Class-A circuits.

During its early years, the Southern Association's chief executives pocketed as much cash as they could before hitting the road, causing a high turnover rate. But in 1903 Judge William Kavanaugh of Little Rock was chosen as president, and through 1915 he did much to shape the destiny of the league. Under Judge John Martin of Memphis (1919–38) the Southern Association would solidify its reputation as the strongest minor league in the National Association.

WAR ON THE HOME FRONT

In 1903, Powell bought out the remaining interest in the Crackers. Over the next two years (in which the Crackers finished fourth and second with him remaining at the helm), Powell made $20,000, a sum so enormous that it roused the jealous ire of local fans who wanted the money for Atlanta, not an outsider.

Thus began a war by the local citizenry against the man who had brought baseball back to Atlanta.

In 1904, a group of powerful politicians decided to run Powell out of town. The city council introduced a bill that would have established a $50 license fee and a five-percent tax on gross team receipts. The bill failed, but the council still levied a $200 license fee and a $100 fee for police protection, and Fulton County laid a $300 assessment on top of that.

Powell's off-the-field problems didn't keep the team from doing well inside the foul lines. In 1904, the Crackers finished second at 78–57 (.578), and ace pitcher Frank Smith rolled up a 31–10 record, thus becoming the league's first 30-game winner.

By then, the team had moved to a field at Piedmont Park, a 189-acre 1,000-seat facility built initially for college athletics and the site of Booker T. Washington's famous "Atlanta Compromise" speech at the 1895 Cotton States and International Exhibition. The park was designed by Frederick Law Olmstead, designer of New York's Central Park and Atlanta's Druid Hills neighborhood. The team had played there since 1902, and had just signed a license to renew its $600 per year contract.

But then the city bought the land for $99,000. A fence was built around the field, the old diamond was demolished and replaced, 1,000 seats were added to the grandstand and separate seats for smokers were built.

Powell, hammered by the city and traction interests, which charged him an additional $5 a game just to guarantee their services, sold the Crackers in 1905 for $20,000 to a syndicate headed by Wally Joyner, fire chief and later mayor of Atlanta. (Powell later would become the Southern Association's "grand old man" as he kept a keen interest in the circuit up to the time of his death in August 1953 at the age of 92.)

Joyner's first act as league president was to hire Otto Jordan as manager. His second was to begin a policy of traveling with his team. "My purpose is to work for the good of Atlanta, and I think I can do more encouraging the home team to do some pennant-winning than I can by sitting in my office at City Hall," he said.

Joyner's first year as owner also saw the outbreak of a deadly yellow-fever epidemic in New Orleans in the middle of the season. The Crescent City was prone to the plague because of its low elevation, the surrounding marshes and extremely high humidity during summer.

Preventive measures against yellow fever were still being developed. Despite playing their remaining games at Chattanooga's Stanton Field, the Pelicans, with former St. Louis Cardinal Charley Frank at the helm, won the pennant that year with an 84–45 (.651) mark. The team finished third at 71–60 (.539).

By then, the Crackers had captured the city's imagination and devotion, and crowds already were overflowing at every Piedmont Park game. Joyner was untiring in his efforts to enlist support to produce a winning ballclub—as well as build an adequate park. In 1906, Joyner convinced Preston Arkwright, president of the Georgia Railway and Electric Company, to buy stock in the team, by arguing that a pennant-winning club that drew good crowds would be an asset to the company by virtue of the travel it would generate.

Arkwright and Joyner then selected a board of directors for themselves: Major Frank Callaway, Gus Ryan and Charles T. Nunnally. The manager of the Atlanta club was turned over to them, with instructions to do whatever was necessary to give Atlanta the best baseball team in the Southern Association.

Their first act was to hire "Tobacco" Billy Smith in 1906 as skipper. Sid Smith of the Crackers won the 1906 batting title with a .326 average. That year the team posted a third-place finish, winning 80 and losing 56 (.588). Tom Hughes was the league's top pitcher, posting a 25–5 record. Another pitcher named Zellner finished with a 24–12 record.

The next step was to begin looking for a new site to play baseball, and the management of the Atlanta Crackers found the ideal spot on a thoroughfare named after a famous Spanish explorer. There they would discover a winning tradition unsurpassed in the annals of minor-league baseball.

27

ST-E-E-E-RIKE!

SECOND INNING

HOME SWEET HOME: THE BIRTH OF PONCEY PARK

Thousands of federal troops held a solid line throughout the city's northeastern section as the Siege of Atlanta raged in the summer of 1864. On a hill where, more than a century later, the first U.S. president from the Deep South would build a library and peace-making enclave, federal troops had a clear view of the Confederacy's heartbeat and watched burn the fires that would finally, once and for all, bring a long and bloody war to an end.

Such was the neighborhood that became the new home of the Atlanta Crackers in 1907, a place where the team would make some history of its own over the decades to come.

Atlanta's Ponce de Leon-Highland community is land rich in Civil War history; historical markers are scattered throughout the area. The residential area was laid out in 1915, and some of the oldest houses still standing were built around 1919 and into the 1920s. Some trees planted along the sidewalks back then still stand along some of the main streets.

The Georgia Railway and Electric Company owned property on Ponce de Leon Avenue directly across the street from an amusement park.

◇

A lake on the site was drained, filled in and converted into a $60,000 ballpark with grandstands made of wood. An opening night crowd of 8,246 welcomed the Crackers to their new home on May 23, 1907. The team responded by winning their first of 17 pennants, finishing the year with a 78–54 record and a .591 winning percentage. Again the hero of the year was Sid Smith, who batted .293 as the club won nine of its last 10 games to win the pennant on the season's final day.

Dode Baskert stole 50 bases, tying Neal Ball of Montgomery for the league stolen-base title. James Fox was another individual champion, topping the league with 62 sacrifice hits. Atlanta had the league's third-highest rated pitcher that year, a thrower named Spade who racked up an impressive 18–12 record.

John Heisman (1869–1936), famed football coach for whom the Downtown Athletic Club named the Heisman Memorial Trophy in 1935, was made president of the Crackers by Georgia Railway & Electric in 1908.

30

In 1908 Georgia Railway & Electric took complete control of the team, and John W. Heisman, one-time team sports director of the Atlanta Athletic Club (later East Lake Golf Club) and then Georgia Tech football coach, was named Cracker president. Tobacco Smith remained as manager as the team finished in sixth place with 63–72, .467. The immortal Tris Speaker, then a 20-year-old Little Rock centerfielder,

Sid Smith cigarette card, issued by American Tobacco Co., circa 1909–11.
Benjamin K. Edwards Collection, Library of Congress

led the league in batting (.350), runs and hits that year, as well as putouts (33) and assists (37) by an outfielder.

THREE CHEERS FOR TOBACCO BILLY

The next year, though, would be a milestone for the Crackers and the Southern Association, as Atlanta led the league in almost every category on their way to a second pennant. Again with Smith at the helm, the team put together a record of 87–49 (640). Dick Bayless was the most-runs-scored champ, 85 in 141 games. Harry Welchonce was the batting champ at .325, a player named Newton was the sacrifice-hit leader (49 in 141 games), and a pitcher named Johns was the league's top thrower, compiling a record of 20–7. Another pitcher, Fisher, went 20–8, and Bill Bartley, a mid-season acquisition from the New Orleans Pelicans, went 19–11 over the course of the season.

"Three Cheers for 'Tobacco' Billy Smith" shouted the headline from the *Atlanta Journal* after the Crackers clinched their second league

The 1907 Crackers won the pennant their inaugural season at Ponce de Leon Ball Park.
Special Collections, Pullen Library, Georgia State University.

◇

A.O. Jordan
cigarette card,
issued by American
Tobacco Co.,
circa 1910.
*Benjamin K. Edwards
Collection, Library of
Congress*

championship. "May he manage the Atlanta club long enough to chew up 40 tons of tobacco and wear out the bottom faces of 50 uniforms sliding up and down the players' bench."

As the Southern Association's 10th season dawned, a young New Orleans player named Joe Jackson was leading the league with a .354 batting average, and the 1910 Atlanta Crackers, under new-old manager Otto Jordan, was finishing third at 75–63 (.543).

HUSTLING EVERY MINUTE OF EVERY PLAY

That year also saw the shortest regulation game (in actual time consumed) in the history of professional baseball, and the Crackers were right in the middle of it.

In a contest all even at 1–1 going into the top of the ninth, the Mobile Gulls scored a run that bested the Crackers. The game was played in Ponce Park on September 19, 1910, and required only 32 minutes to complete. Apparently there was a desire on the part of the players to show how quickly a game could actually be played. Both teams hustled every minute of the way, and they didn't wait out the pitchers but rather swung at all the good pitches to eliminate any waste of time.

The pitchers, Chappell of Mobile and Griffin of Atlanta, were getting the ball over the plate; Chappell walked the only batter of the game. Not one player struck out. Both clubs were hitting to the infield far more than average, as Mobile first baseman Swacina had

17 putouts against 15 for Peter Lister of Atlanta. In the end, Mobile scored six hits against Atlanta's four.

In 1911, Georgia Railway & Electric put the Atlanta Crackers up for sale, with an asking price of $40,000. Former owner Wally Joyner put together a small syndicate of buyers, but couldn't raise nearly enough money. Several executives at the Coca-Cola Co. expressed some interest, despite the fact that Coke's chief competitor, the Red Rock Ko-nit Co., had exclusive rights to distribute its beverage at Ponce de Leon Ball Park.

But even these high-ranking Coke executives couldn't find enough interested buyers to come up with the cash, and the team remained on the block for several years. And judging from the 1911 Crackers' record, the team may have been distracted by these off-the-field happenings, as they finished in last place with a miserable record of 54–94 (.391). The following year wasn't much better, as Charles Hemphill's managerial debut resulted in a cellar-dwelling 54–83 performance (.394).

Despite their last-place finish, several Crackers did end the season leading the Southern Association in various categories. Welchonce was the league batting champ at .325, and King Bailey was the most-runs scored leader with 89. On September 4, Cracker hurler Ray Bressler may have had something on the ball besides excellent control. On that day, Bressler pitched only 72 balls to win a nine-inning game against the Nashville Vols.

THEY JUST UP AND QUIT

The team was still up for sale in 1913, but that year the Atlanta Crackers set the Southern Association on fire. With "Tobacco" Billy Smith back at the helm, the team won 22 of their last 23 games, a .957 winning percentage. And they captured the pennant on the last day by a half-game over the Mobile Gulls.

Tommy Long scored 112 runs in 140 games, giving him

33

the league scoring title. Billy Smith hit 16 triples that year, more than anyone else. A pitcher named Price was the third-winningest thrower in the league, posting a 20–9 record, as Atlanta posted an overall 81–56 (.591) record.

The winning streak began on August 16, the eighteenth day of Atlanta's notorious Leo Frank-Mary Phagan murder trial. The Crackers beat the Lookouts 7–2 and over the next 22 games Atlanta would lose only once, on August 30, to New Orleans 7–5. Mobile had a five-and-a-half game lead over the Crackers with only seven days left in the season, and they were faced with a four-game set in the Crackers' backyard. They were then set to finish the season against the last-place Pelicans.

Over three days, 26,926 people attended the games, a new Southern Association record. Atlanta beat the Gulls in the first two games, 4–1 and 4–3, with a massive doubleheader on Friday afternoon. The Crackers won the first in a 10-inning nailbiter, 6–5. Then, with a scoreless tie in the third inning of the second game, Mobile manager Mike Finn suddenly took his team off the field. His explanation? It was time for the train to leave that would take his team back to Alabama.

The Crackers and their fans were livid, and some fans even volunteered to pay for a specially chartered train after the game was over. But Finn was within his rights. According to league rules, a team was not obligated to complete a game when the specified time to depart arrived. And Finn probably figured that his team's chances of beating the last-place Pelicans were better than against the red-hot Atlantans.

"Atlanta so completely humiliated the Mobile stars in every department that the team lost its fight and quit cold," exclaimed the *Atlanta Constitution* the next day.

Still enraged, the Crackers walloped the hapless Lookouts in their next game 5–0. But the Gulls, as Finn gambled, defeated New Orleans 4–3 in their first game against the Pelicans. That left both the Gulls and the Crackers with identical records of 81–56 on the season's last day. The Crackers had already played their last game, and some of the players, dismissing their chances of winning a pennant, were taking their leave by train.

From 3:00 P.M. until 7:00 P.M. on the season's last day, as the Gulls played the Pelicans, the *Atlanta Journal* received detailed accounts of the contest via about 20 telephone lines. When word came in that the Pelicans had defeated the Gulls 5–2, the city went wild.

And those Cracker players had to be pulled off their respective trains, because the Southern Association champions were scheduled to play a benefit game the next day against Knoxville, the Appalachian League champs!

FOR SALE NO LONGER

The Crackers came off that championship high in 1914, as a fourth-place (78–66, .542) finish awaited Tobacco Smith and his charges. The year's only highlight was the performance of pitcher Oscar Dent, who set an all-time league record for most innings pitched without a base-on-ball, 63. Much of the nation's baseball fan base was captured that year by the debut of the Federal League, a short and eventually ill-fated attempt to challenge the supremacy of the National League. That year also saw the brief emergence of a players union at the major league level, called the Fraternity of Professional Base Ball Players, an organization that vanished with the Federal League.

Meanwhile, the Crackers still had a "For Sale" sign hanging on them. Finally, in 1915, Atlanta Councilman Frank Reynolds and J.W. Goldsmith Jr., son of a former city councilman and the nephew of the city comptroller, bought the Crackers for

$37,000. Unfortunately, the players failed to respond with any enthusiasm to their new owners, as evidenced by a fifth-place record of 74–79 (.483.) Roy Moran was the only player to put up any meaningful numbers, leading the league with 20 triples in 152 games.

After the 1915 campaign, Smith was fired and replaced by Charley Frank, who only slightly improved over his predecessor with a 70–67 (.511) fifth-place record. Atlanta's Scott Perry pitched more innings than any other thrower in 1916, 336.

With most of the same players returning for the next season, the Atlanta Crackers gave no sign, at least during spring training of 1917, of returning to any semblance of championship form. Yet the Crackers would set another milestone in the Southern Association: the first team to win 90 or more games.

So much for first impressions.

Frank led his team to an overall 98–56 (.636) record and a fourth pennant. Moran had 177 hits in 157 games, while Rube Bressler went 25–15 on the mound. The 1917 version racked up more hits and runs than any previous Cracker team and never lost a series against an opposing team. But true to form, the team went through another post-championship letdown in 1918, finishing in last place with a World War I-shortened record of 18–49 (.269).

STEAMBOAT AND THE LAWMAN

The next year the Crackers rebounded with a 85–53 (.616) record, with Charlie Frank still at the controls. A group of young, powerful players was nicknamed the "Arsenic Brigade." The cadre included infielders Jimmy Dykes, Chick Galloway, Ivy Griffin, Sammy Mayer and Bob Higgins, and pitching greats Johnny Suggs and Tom Sheehan, who had the lowest ERA in the league that year, 1.68.

Before a Poncey crowd of 15,000, infielder Dykes—later to become a

The *New York Daily News* reported that Steamboat Johnson had not missed a single assignment during his 27 seasons in the Southern Association—more than 4,400 games. He called 10 Dixie World Series and every Southern All-Star game from the beginning of the contest in 1938 until he retired in 1946.

traveled major-league manager—clinched the Crackers franchise's fifth pennant with a two-run double into the crowd. A full two weeks were left in the season.

Besides a remarkably successful season for the Atlanta Crackers, 1919 (a year in which, with the Chicago White Sox accused of throwing the World Series against the Cincinnati Reds, the long arm of the law reached into the national pastime more than any other time in history) also saw the only instance in recorded baseball annals when a manager filed a legal injunction to remove an opposing pitcher from the mound. Mobile was playing in Atlanta in the last game of a three-game set, and the famed umpire Harry "Steamboat" Johnson was the man in blue.

"Bob Hasty was pitching for the Bears, and the game was going along fine, when a man in plain clothes came walking out toward the pitcher's mound," Johnson recalled in his 1935 autobiography, *Standing the Gaff*. The umpire called "time" and rushed out to the mound. The man "stated that he was the law, showed me his badge and a warrant for Hasty," Johnson wrote.

37

Frank had taken out an injunction in court to keep Hasty from pitching!

"You have no right on this field," Johnson said. "I am running this game and will stand for no interference from the law or anything else." The officer told Johnson that he couldn't remove a lawman from the field and only after Johnson threatened to forfeit the game to Mobile did the man return to the grandstands, saying he would wait for Hasty outside the park when the game was over.

"In some way, exact details of which I never learned, Hasty slipped out of the park by a side gate, into a taxicab and rushed down to the [train] station where he was locked in a drawing room on the Mobile Pullman car," Johnson wrote. "None of us ever heard of that warrant again."

Johnson would become one of the most famous names in umpiring history. He began his career in 1909 and, except for 1914, when he umpired in the National League, and 1921 in the South Atlantic League, remained in the Southern Association until his retirement after the '46 season. He became a beloved figure on the circuit, and always carried a document made out by a recognized eye doctor that certified his vision as 20/20, in the event fans ever questioned his eyesight.

Johnson picked up his famous moniker in 1919 during his first trip to Atlanta, in which he took the city's press by storm. Until then he had been known as Bulldog Johnson.

"In those days before the loudspeakers came into use, the umpire had to announce the batteries," Johnson wrote. "After I had brushed off the [home] plate, I called out the batteries in my usual voice, which I guess was pretty deep and loud."

The next day, *Atlanta Georgian* sports editor Ed Danforth wrote "none of us know where [Southern Association president] John D.

Martin got this Umpire Johnson, but he has a voice like a Mississippi steamboat. From now he is 'Steamboat' Johnson to Atlantans," as he would become to the rest of the league as well.

The *Atlanta Journal* also jumped on Steamboat's bandwagon that year. "When he announces the batteries he reaches far down into his lungs and sweeps his voice all around the stands," reported the paper. "He twists his mouth and gesticulates like a Fourth of July orator delighting the multitudes from the elevation of a soap box." And, as the *Atlanta Constitution* put it, "there have been umpires and just plain umps, boobs and scientific decision-makers at Ponce de Leon park, but until Monday afternoon Atlanta had never been honored by such an umpire as the one who put in an appearance in the person of Harry S. Johnson."

Atlanta's Krehmyer is out at first and Mobile's first baseman Robert "Ray" Knode looks to umpire Steamboat Johnson to call it correctly.

KILL THE UMP!

Johnson umpired in an era when "Kill the ump!" was more than just a rhetorical threat. He and his brothers in blue faced serious physical danger every time they walked onto a diamond. They were beaten with fists, bombarded with flying glassware and occasionally assaulted with lethal weapons. Homicides were not uncommon.

"I have rendered one million decisions since I began

39

umpiring in 1909," Johnson wrote in *Standing the Gaff.* "Something like 4,000 bottles have been thrown at me in my day, but only about 20 ever hit me. That does not speak well for the accuracy of the fans' throwing."

But of all the bottle showers Johnson endured, the worst came in 1919 in Atlanta—"a city in which fans are usually very orderly and treat players and umpires fairly," Johnson wrote. "It was on a holiday and Mobile was playing. In the 11th inning I had to put [Crackers] Bob Higgins, catcher, and Ray Roberts, pitcher, out of the game at once. The sight of an umpire firing their battery all at once infuriated the fans. There were around 15,000 present, and it looked as if every one must have had a bottle in his hand. For there came a shower of bottles that beat anything I ever experienced.

"The Atlanta fans were good throwers too."

Johnson was hit several times in the back and head, but was not knocked out. Police escorted him into the dressing room under the stands. As he began to shower, someone fired a shot through a window right above the showerhead. Johnson happened to be bending down to wash his feet at the time, so the bullet missed his head.

"The police, who were standing by inside the room, ran outside, but in the crowd of several hundred they could not locate who had fired the shot," Johnson wrote. "Neither were the officers able to break up the crowd, so they took me out the back gate, and I arrived at [the] hotel with no more adventures.

"The first man to talk to me after I arrived at the hotel was Bill Cody, the chief of the fire department. . . . Cody was a fine sportsman, and he came in to apologize for the way Atlanta had treated me, but I told him I held no resentment toward them at all."

THE LONGEST GAME

Steamboat Johnson also umpired the longest game in Southern Association history on June 13, 1919, when the Crackers played the Lookouts in Chattanooga. Atlanta was in first place and the Lookouts were dead last. The hero and goat of this record-breaking game was pitcher Rube Marshall of the Lookouts. In 23 innings, he allowed only 16 hits and two runs. He struck out 23 Crackers and didn't walk a man. In addition he had three hits, while Ray Roberts pitched the entire game for the Atlanta Crackers.

That's the "hero stuff." Here's the "goat angle."

The Lookouts should have won the game in 19 innings, 3–2. The honor of scoring the winning run should have been credited to one of the Lookouts' outfielders, a player named Lacey. However, a colossal error on the part of Marshall voided the winning run and sent the contest into extra innings four more times, when Johnson finally called the game on account of darkness.

In the 19th inning, with the bases loaded and two out, Griffin, the Lookouts' leadoff man, singled sharply to the outfield and the game was apparently over. From third base, Lacey crossed home plate with what appeared to be the winning run. However, Marshall was on first when Griffin hit. Marshall, instead of running to second base, left the field and rushed toward the Chattanooga clubhouse, all while the Crackers were playing out the string. The ball was thrown back to the infield and Atlanta's second baseman held it on second, making a forced third out and erasing the hit and the run along with it. Lacey, the runner at third, had crossed the plate long before Marshall was forced at second. However, that meant nothing since no run can score on a forced third out.

Jimmy Dykes had a busy day at second for Atlanta. He

41

handled 22 chances without an error, and posted 11 putouts and 11 assists.

THE BLAZING 20s

As the 1920s dawned, the first Cracker team of the decade arguably had as much, if not more, talent than any other club to that point behind manager Dick Kaufmann. Pitcher Tom Sheehan (who took a turn in 1960 as manager of the major-league Giants) won 26 games and lost 17, the last time an Atlanta thrower would win as many as 25.

Sheehan also set an all-time league record for pitching the most innings in one game. On June 26, in the first game of a doubleheader, he won a nine-inning game against Little Rock, 5–1. The second game ended in a 15-inning tie. All totalled, Sheehan pitched an incredible 24 innings that day.

Still, the 1920 Crackers finished third with a record of 85–72 (.578), despite the presence of such other eternal Atlanta favorites as Dick Burrus, Ben Paschal (who later played with Babe Ruth for seven seasons with the Yankees) and Benny Karr. Johnny Suggs (father of future pro golfer Louise Suggs) would make his presence felt on the Atlanta mound in 1921, when he pitched a no-hitter against Memphis. Charley Frank had returned to the captain's chair, but could do no better than leading his team to a fifth-place, 73–78 (.483) finish.

A year later, the record was even worse. New skipper Roy Ellam and the '22 Crackers finished dead last, 55–97 (.362). The glory days of the Atlanta Crackers were fading, and fading fast. Otto Miller managed the '23 team, which finished fourth at 78–73 (.516). Two players did have outstanding seasons, as Danny Clark, a mid-season acquisition from Birmingham, led the league with 19 homers, and Oscar Tuero led the league with 89 sacrifice hits.

42

Then tragedy struck the organization on September 9, 1923, a calamity from which the finest park in minor-league baseball would arise, a facility that would also house some of minor-league base-ball's greatest teams and enduring moments.

BALL FOUR!

THIRD INNING

THE FINEST PARK IN THE MINORS

While the whole scene was lit up with noonday brilliance, the snapping of high wires from time to time suddenly changed the lighting to a bluish hue. Billboards on the side of the park, fence posts, even the leaves of the trees were burning and sending myriads of sparks into the air, showering the neighboring trees with a rain of fire. While the whole area was a raging furnace, the center of the park, situated in the center of the valley, became the scene of a flaming whirlwind.

So the *Atlanta Constitution* described the scene at Ponce de Leon Park on September 9, 1923. Flames shot 100 feet high, and telephone poles along the street became pillars of fire, as Ponce de Leon Ball Park was completely destroyed by fire, the cause of which remains unknown to this day.

What was known was that $75,000 worth of damage had been done. All of the Cracker uniforms, team records and trophies were lost. Almost lost was team secretary "Silver" Bill Stickney, who was asleep in his quarters under the grandstands when the fire started. He was rescued, but suffered severe burns all over his body.

But then, striding through this path of destruction, came a man whose greatest desire in life was to build the most glorious baseball park in the nation, and leave it behind as a legacy to his name.

Rell Jackson Spiller was a heavyset man who was never to be seen in public without a hat. A wealthy concessionaire, he wanted to build a gift to posterity, so he shelled out a total outlay of $250,000 to build a concrete-and-steel baseball park on a 23-acres site that would put anything else in the Southern Association to shame. Even the Pacific Coast League with such cities as San Francisco and Los Angeles on the circuit didn't have a stadium that could compare with the palatial monument towering in R.J. Spiller's dreams.

The Crackers finished out the '23 season at Georgia Tech's Grant Field, until their newly redesigned and rebuilt home could be completed. When R.J. Spiller Field made its debut in time for the 1924 season, Atlanta's *City Builder* newspaper called it "the most magnificent park in the minor leagues."

"That, in the expert opinion of major- and minor-league sportswriters, scouts and players themselves," the paper wrote, "is the easiest and most fitting description of the mammoth R.J. Spiller Field, newly erected in the spot where the old dilapidated wooden stands formerly stood."

Indeed, the new facility drew lavish praise from the likes of Branch Rickey, then-manager of the St. Louis Cardinals; Southern Association president John D. Martin; Larry Gilbert, manager of the New Orleans Pelicans; and numerous other major-league scouts and reporters. Chairs were fastened into the stadium's new concrete skeleton, seats that were far more comfortable than the benches Atlanta fans used to occupy. The grandstand's entire capacity was 9,800. The bleachers for whites, located in right field, accommodated 2,500 with an equal number of grandstand seats in left field for black fans. Birmingham's Rickwood Field was second to Spiller's in terms of capacity, and that was 4,000 less.

On opening days and holidays, Spiller Field could hold 20,000 fans,

Appropriate for the Phoenix City, Ponce de Leon Ball Park, shown here in a 1920s postcard, arose from the ashes of an eponymous field on the same location.

there being enough standing room for more than 6,000. The fence was 365 feet down the left-field line, 321 to right and a Herculean 462 to dead center, where a giant magnolia tree stood. (Spiller Field had the only ground rules in baseball history allowing for a tree in the out-field. Babe Ruth, in a pre-season barnstorming tour, and future Hall of Famer Eddie Mathews are the only two men ever verified to have hit home run balls into a magnolia.)

GIRLS, HORSES AND ALLIGATORS

Spiller Field had a manually operated scoreboard, at least in the beginning. As a boy, Henry Bowden, now a prominent Atlanta attorney, used to climb that left center scoreboard . . . a lot.

47

"We had a fellow named Doc Auten sitting in the press box, and he wore a radio headset," Bowden recalled. "I wore a headset also, and he'd radio for me to change the numbers on the scoreboard for runs, ball, strikes and outs. So I'd climb up a ladder and drop a new and different number in the respective slots." Bowden also sold refreshments at the park, shouting "Peee-nuts, cig-ars, cig-a-rettes and chewing gum!" or "Co-Cola, lemon, orange and grape here!"

A former Standard & Hood Oil Company employee would become a legendary fixture at Spiller Field: E.H. "Fat" Elrod. Bowden recalled, "In front of home plate, he'd walk around in a white smock with his name on the back, and use a giant megaphone to shout 'Line-ups for today's game . . .' Then he'd rumble, 'Play ball!,' and the Crackers would run onto the field."

The park made for a great show. Next door, outside the third-base line, was a public swimming pool so if the game got a little slow, the boys could go watch the girls swimming. The Southern Railroad tracks ran behind the first-base line, and engineers sometimes stopped their iron-clad carriages to take in a little baseball action.

"Across the street was a bunch of horse stables," said longtime Atlanta sports fan Joe Gerson. "There also was a Gulf filling station nearby. Spiller also owned a restaurant next door to the park where he sponsored alligator wrestling."

"ONE DOLLAR HE DOESN'T FOUL THE BALL!"

Besides all of this, fans at Cracker games could entertain themselves with another pastime. Georgia law allowed gambling when it wasn't conducted under a roof, so while the covered grandstands became home to the true Cracker faithful, the outfield bleachers were host to the "fly ball fans" who sat with the local oddsmakers.

Often bookies gave 8-to-1 odds for a double and 20-to-1 for a homer. Bowden said, "bookies would stand up with a fistful of dollars

48

Crackers outfielder Wilbur Goode at bat. In 1925, Goode set a Southern Association record for most hits with 236 and won the SA batting championship with .379. *Atlanta History Center*

in their hands and say 'one dollar to one-and-a-half if he does not foul the ball!'" Many fans would put up 50 cents and, if any of the outfielders caught a fly ball, the bookie paid off $2.50. When an outfielder for an opposing team dropped a fly ball he should have caught, the grandstands went wild, while unmerciful boos and hisses came from the "fly ball" bleachers.

Buster Cheatham was a shortstop for the Crackers in the 20s, and he probably saved bookies more money than any minor leaguer in history with his spectacular outfield catches. Once a group of bookies even gave him a pot of about $200 in appreciation. Chatham, afraid that people would think he'd been corrupted, gave it back.

Soon, Cracker officials began prohibiting gambling during games. No matter—the bookies and their customers

49

Frank Zoeller led the Southern Association in runs scored in 1925 with 131.
Atlanta History Center

50 simply devised another language: hand signals. One or two fingers signified certain bets, and while the police frantically patrolled the stands looking for perpetrators, the bookies were paying or collecting from their customers. One story even has it that a well-dressed businessman sitting in the outfield bleachers was holding up a couple of fingers, trying to make change with a vendor, when the police threw him out of the park under suspicion of gambling.

The team, meanwhile, now with player/manager Bert Niehoff at the helm, broke in their new home with a second-place finish in 1924 (99–54, .647). Ben Paschal led the league in runs scored, 136. J. Carlysle "Red" Smith, hero of the 1914 miracle Boston Braves, won the batting title with a .385 average.

In 1925, with most of the '24 team returning, Niehoff and the team came home with a sixth Cracker pennant. Wilbur Goode won the batting title with a .379 average and 236 hits, the best of any Cracker in team history. Right fielder Frank Zoeller led the league with 131 runs scored.

During spring training, pitching coach Dan Michalove had put together one of the most impressive arrays of pitchers ever assembled by a minor-league club. The rest of the Southern Association club owners yelled loudly about Michalove's supposed buying of a pennant and his solid-gold pitching staff became a controversy. But this high-priced throwing crew pretty much went bust, as most of them folded up with sore arms or injuries. Michalove then had to recruit a completely new lineup of odds and ends from the remnant

Nick Cullop, Crackers outfielder, receives a hat full of money after hitting a home run. Cullop led the Southern Association in 1925 hitting 30 home runs in 137 games, despite the tragic death of his young son that year. *Atlanta History Center*

51

counter, and the team's reward was a first-place finish at 87–67 (.565). George Pipgras (19–15) and Harold McLaughlin (19–13), two of those pitching rejects, were the Southern Association's second- and third-winningest throwers that year.

In 1925 centerfielder Nick Cullop became one of the most beloved Crackers of all time for reasons of personal tragedy off the field as well as his exploits on it. Shortly after breakfast on July 4, Cullop's young son Billy fell through a window screen in the family's third-floor apartment to the pavement below, breaking his neck and killing him instantly. Cullop was at Spiller Field that morning, practicing for an afternoon game. According to the *Atlanta Constitution,* "dazed and grief-stricken, he dashed frantically out of the dressing room and, without taking time to hail a taxi or anything, ran all the way home at top speed, where he collapsed."

Grief-stricken, Cullop lost 14 pounds and didn't play for two weeks. But when he did return, he hit 30 baseballs out of Southern Association parks over the rest of the season, all in memory of his son.

ONLY IN AMERICA

R.J. Spiller became sole owner of the Atlanta Crackers in the summer of 1926, and retained the sold rights to the club until he made a quarter of a million dollars. Where else on the face of the globe could a man have sold enough peanuts and soda pop to have become the sole owner of a franchise worth $267,000? Only in America.

Spiller's first season as owner was marked by a team with a pitching staff reputed to be as good as any in the league. Ray Francis, a blond southpaw, came to spring training in great shape and was projected to be the association's leading lefty. Longtime player Pug Cavet was still being counted on to produce. Cliff Markie and Ruel Love

Hall of Famer Leo Durocher, shown in Atlanta in 1926, played shortstop for the Crackers. *Tracey O'Neal Collection, Pullen Library, Georgia State University.*

were predicted to win big that year, and Tennessean Tom Rogers, "the Gallatin Gunner," was to be the staff's ace right-hander.

Among the promising newcomers were George Johnston, an old Auburn University pitcher; Pete Fowler, a South Atlantic League lefthander on whom fine reports had been received; and Raoul Alvarez, a Cuban unknown in the U.S. but who nonetheless had nice motions and considerable speed. But Atlanta could manage only a poor fifth-place finish (75–76, .497) in 1926, just one year after they'd won the pennant. Despite that disappointing season, they entered 1927 optimistic, with Niehoff going on record as being determined to give Atlanta a winning club "if it takes the last cent in Rell Jackson Spiller's safe."

Niehoff was a shrewd manager who had finished worse

53

than second only once since entering the Southern Association six years prior. He had excellent connections with major-league clubs through personal friendships with managers dating from the days he played with the Phillies and Reds.

Any minor-league manager was glad to farm a recruit with Bert Niehoff, so assured were they that the player would get plenty of good instruction. The Crackers had an outfield composed of Frank Zoeller, Mule Haas and Frank Welch. Defensively it was the equal of any team in the league. Niehoff was hoping Welch, an old Philadelphia Athletics star, would supply the long-ball hitting punch.

The pitching staff again was reputed to be the best in the league, and Memphis standby Frank Kohlbecker and Johnny Brock were two of the smartest backstops in the minors. Neither was a heavy hitter, but Kohlbecker was a very dangerous man to have up with men on base. He had a flair for scoring base hits when runs were needed. During the '24 season, he played with Memphis, and almost single-handedly beat Atlanta out of the pennant.

The left wing of the infield found Walter Gilbert at third and Manuel Cueto, formerly with Mobile, at short. Gilbert was a polished defensive player and a good hitter. Cueto was a good shortstop and a selfless team player. He was the hit-and-run man in the lineup, batting second. Rod Murphy played first base, but preferred the utility man's role.

Despite all of that talent, another fifth-place finish (70–81, .464) awaited the team at the end of the 1927 season, and the Crackers were heading backwards again—*fast*. When the Southern Association adopted a split-season format in 1928, Niehoff posted a 31–41 (.431) record at the break and was replaced by former Cracker star player Wilbur Goode, who didn't do much better (34–46, .432).

In a season with few highlights (Jim Poole led the league with 42 doubles), there were plenty of lowlights, the worst being the longest single-day losing streak in baseball history. One day in June 1928, league president Martin ruled that Atlanta must forfeit 14 games because the organization had violated an obscure player-classification rule regarding how much amateur playing time constituted a player being designated as a rookie.

By then the Crackers were getting used to finishing toward the cellar of the standings. Goode could manage no better than yet another fifth-place, 78–75 (.510) record in '29. Poole led the league with 127 RBIs, and also was the year's home-run (17) champ. Pitcher "Climax" Blethen (so named for the ever-present wad of Climax Plug Chewing Tobacco in his jaw) went 22–11, the league's second-rated tosser.

IN NEED OF EXPERIENCE

Johnny Dobbs, a Chattanooga native, once had been a speedy outfielder for Cincinnati, Chicago and Brooklyn in the National League from 1901 to 1905. After his playing days were over, he managed Nashville in 1907, Chattanooga in 1910, Montgomery from 1911–13, New Orleans from 1914–22, Memphis from 1923–24, and Birmingham from 1925–29. Over those periods of time he led his teams to five pennants: two for New Orleans, one in Memphis and two with Birmingham.

If any man was going to turn the Crackers' fortunes around, it would be none other than Johnny Dobbs, right? Well, after a fourth-place finish in 1930 as the Crackers' new manager (84–69, .549) and a sixth-place finish (78–76, .506) in 1931, Dobbs' professional career in the Southern Association came to an end. (Over his career, Dobbs ranks statistically second only to Larry Gilbert in longevity among Southern Association managers. He compiled a record of 1,841 victories against 1,452 losses for a .559 percentage.)

Dobbs' years in Atlanta did produce a few good individual numbers for some players. In 1930 future Cooperstown resident Luke Appling began his baseball career with the

55

North Carolina-born Luke Appling
began his career with the Crackers
his sophomore year at Oglethorpe
University. At the end of the 1930
season, Chicago paid Atlanta $20,000
for his contract. He served as a part-
time minor-league hitting instructor
for the Atlanta Braves from the
1970s—1990 and died in 1991
in Cumming, Ga.
National Baseball Hall of Fame Library

Crackers, playing in 104 games
and finishing with a .326 average.
(Appling went on to a 20-year
career with the Chicago White
Sox, batting .310 lifetime over
2,218 games. His average was
.444 in All-Star games. In 1936

and 1943 he won the American League batting titles, .388 and
.328, respectively).

The 1931 leader in triples was Doug Taitt, with 19. Blethen, with
a 20–11 record, was the third-winningest pitcher in the league. On
June 10, against the Little Rock Travelers, second baseman Jack
Sheehan set an all-time league record of most assists in a game for a
second sacker, 13.

With former Cracker star David Irenus "Red" Barron hired to take
over in 1932, Atlanta finished seventh, with a record of 62–90 (.408).
The only high point of the year was a five-game win streak by Bob
Hasty against the Nashville Volunteers, the Chattanooga Lookouts
and the Knoxville Smokies on July 17, 19, 24, 26 and 28. (Hasty was
the Mobile Gulls pitcher against whom Cracker manager Charley
Frank had taken out an injunction in 1919.)

For the most part, though, the Crackers were going nowhere. By then, Spiller had sold the team to Robert Woodruff and the Coca-Cola Co., and the team's new owners were not about to stand by and do nothing while the team continued to lose. Thus they began a search for new baseball talent who would turn the team's fortunes around. In doing so, the Atlanta Crackers rediscovered a young baseball man who began his career selling peanuts as a boy at Spiller Field. In 1933 they hired him as assistant general manager, marking his return to Atlanta where he would become a legend.

LINE DRIVE!!

FOURTH INNING

A MANN WHO LOVED THE THEATER

"I'm just one of those fellows that good fortune gave a lot of energy to and I don't feel right if I'm not using it. I've got no secrets about what success I've had. All I've got to show for it is a lot of long hours and I was putting them in at an age when most kids are only worrying about what they're going to get for Christmas."

—Earl Mann

F irst the smile—bright and wide—that can only belong to a man who delights in living. Then the hairline that started heading south when he was only 17. Finally, the clear, deep eyes that offer just a hint of the steely business sense that lies within.

Those were the first things one saw when one cast eyes on Earl Mann, and they created an indelible impression even when seen across the chasm of time from an old, wrinkled, yellowing newspaper clip. Known as the "Baseball Genius in Dixie" and "Mr. Atlanta Baseball," Mann rose from humble beginnings as a Georgia farm boy to the builder of a baseball dynasty.

Earl Mann was general manager of the Crackers from 1933 until 1947 when he purchased the team. Mr. Atlanta Baseball relinquished control of the team to the Southern Association in 1959.
National Baseball Hall of Fame Library

Mann was born October 2, 1904, in the small town of Riverdale, just south of downtown Atlanta. Even before he finished Atlanta Tech High School, his baseball career was underway—he sold peanuts, seat cushions and soft drinks at Spiller Field at the tender age of 12.

Mann's education continued not only at north Atlanta's Oglethorpe University (where he was a pretty fair pitcher for the Petrels), but also in the theater. "My father loved the theater," said Oreon Mann, Earl's only son. "He grew up in the theater as an usher and at the time he first went into baseball—not just as a peanut vendor but in ticket sales too—he was holding another job at the O'Lyrick Theater downtown. He had a chance to become head usher, but he wanted to go into baseball.

"He was told he was making a big mistake."

In 1920, Mann was promoted to selling war-tax tickets at the ballpark. He became assistant team secretary in 1924, and it wasn't long before the "assistant" was dropped. Mann stayed with the Crackers until 1929.

Then he took off to become farm-team business manager for the

Brooklyn Dodgers' minor-league club in Rocky Mount, N.C. The team won a pennant, and the Dodgers promoted him to general manager of the Macon Peaches, where his team won a pennant. Mann then moved to the Hartford (Conn.) Senators, where his team also won a pennant. In 1932, the Yankees hired him away to be the general manager of its Wheeling Stogies farm team in Wheeling, W. Va., where the team again won a pennant.

Earl Mann had gone four-for-four in the pennant category over four years.

THE STORY OF THE FIVE WIRES

Coca-Cola bought the Crackers in 1933, and hired Mann to be an assistant to "Uncle" Wilbert Robinson, an old Brooklyn Dodger who was serving as general manager. But in 1934, Robinson suddenly and unexpectedly passed away. According to Oreon Mann, Coke president Robert Woodruff was in Paris at the time. Hughes Spalding, lawyer for both Coke and the Crackers, wired Woodruff, asking; "What do I do?"

Woodruff wired back: "Take over."

An exchange followed—

Spalding: "I'm too old. I hired Mann."

Woodruff: "Mann is too young. You take over."

Spalding: "Mann may be too young but I'm too old. Mann's got it."

The new general manager was only 29. With Woodruff's financial backing and Mann's baseball savvy, the Atlanta Crackers would develop into the Southern Association's premier team. (On the day that Ponce de Leon Ball Park was auctioned off, Mann would recall that his appointment as general manager of the Atlanta Crackers was "my most thrilling memory.")

Mann was among the first minor-league operators to

61

send scouts, or "bird dogs," throughout other baseball parks, looking for talent. After a player was recruited, Mann paid him between $1,000 and $2,500 up front and wrote into the player's contract a provision that the player would be paid a percentage of what Mann made if the athlete was sold to the majors.

"Earl Mann was a tremendous person, on my all-time top-10 list of the best," said Jesse Outlar, who covered the Crackers for the *Atlanta Constitution*. "He was a big guy with tremendous charisma and personality. Every player knew that if Earl sold him to the bigs, he'd give him a cut of the take."

A BALL PLAYER'S OWNER

"He was a ball player's owner," said Ralph "Country" Brown, who went to the Crackers in the late 1940s. "We'd be playing a game and if anybody made a big play to save the game or got the base hit to win the game, Earl Mann was waiting at the gate when you'd come out. He made sure to shake your hand and there'd be something in his hand, too. He loved his players and took care of them."

Mann could sit in his office at Poncey and watch the games. "To get to the press box, you had to walk up a long ramp, and you passed by Mann's office," Outlar said. "He had a porthole in his office that gave him a direct view of the field." And that vantage point gave the Crackers' new general manager and future team owner a view of some of the best minor-league teams in history.

In 1933, Mann's first year on the job, the Southern Association adopted another split-season format, and this time it featured a championship playoff series between the two half-season winners. Atlanta, managed by Charley Moore, finished in sixth place over the first half (37–40, .481) and dead last in the second (25–46, .352), despite the fact that Hawaiian star "Prince" Henry Oana led the league in homers (17).

62

POWER AT THE PLATE

For a team to end the year with a losing record, the Crackers displayed incredible power behind the plate.

They went on a batting spree in a three-game series with the Nashville Volunteers staged May 26–28. The Crackers scored 45 runs on 61 hits but could do no better than win two of the three games. They scored 19 runs in the first game, 15 in the second game and 11 in the third battle of bats. However, the Volunteers scored 19 runs in the third contest, eking out a victory. Atlanta had 25 hits in the first affair, 19 in the second and 17 in the last.

The team's overall record was only slightly better the next year, with Spencer Abbott holding the reins. The team came in third (37–33, .529) and fifth (40–41, .494) over the season's first and second halves.

The longest game in Southern Association history—in terms of how many days it took to complete it—took place that year, and again the Crackers were involved (the team already had played in the league's shortest and longest games). On August 18 against Little Rock, after three innings of play, the game was stopped because of rain. Replayed on the 25th, rain again suspended hostilities with the score tied 5–5. Atlanta finally won it in 11 innings 5–4 on August 27, when the game was finally finished.

THE GRAND SLAM—SOUTHERN-STYLE

For 1935 Southern officials scrapped the split-season format in favor of the Shaughnessy plan, a popular playoff format spreading rapidly through the minors as a means of sustaining fan interest throughout the season. Frank "Shag" Shaughnessy, general manager of the International League's Montreal Royals, persuaded the league to begin utilizing his plan two years earlier.

The scheme called for the top four teams in the league to

Gerard Lipscomb leads off for the Crackers while Lee Head catches for the Smokies before a crowd of 18,671 in the 1935 opener.

compete in a playoff series at the end of the season. The first- and fourth-place teams, and the second- and third-place teams would each play in a best three-out-of-five series, and the two winning teams would advance to the finals in another three-for-five set. In later years a four-out-of-seven format would be used.

The Southern Association added its own unique little twist to the Shaughnessy playoffs when it decided to award the first-place finisher $1,000, an amount that was increased to $2,500 in 1934. The league also made arrangements for the Shaughnessy champion to play the pennant-winner in the Texas League in a playoff set called the Dixie Series. Capturing the league pennant, winning the Shaughnessy play-offs and then triumphing in the Dixie Series was hitting the Southern Association grand slam, and the Atlanta Crackers would do it more times than any other team in history.

Mann appointed Eddie Moore as manager in 1935 and he

responded by winning not only the pennant (91–60, .605) but the first Shaughnessies. ERA champ Harry Kelley (23–13) and L.B. Thomas (20–16) were tops on the mound, and first baseman Alex Hooks (.341) led the league in batting. The '35 team was plenty tough to score on, as they allowed only 593 runs to be scored against them throughout the year.

On May 3, the Crackers' Dave Harris scored three triples against Nashville. On May 14, against the Lookouts, the Crackers won an extra-inning game the weird way when, in the 12th inning, they scored three runs on two base-on-balls and two errors courtesy of Chattanooga.

The Crackers swept the fourth-place Nashville Vols in round one of the playoffs, and in the finals breezed by the New Orleans Pelicans. Atlanta set a then-league-attendance record as 330,000 fans passed through Poncey's turnstiles in 1935, more than one-third of the Southern's total draw that year. Although the Crackers lost to the Oklahoma City Indians in the Dixie Series four games to two, 26,000 fans turned out for the three games at Poncey, as opposed to only 17,000 in Oklahoma City.

A NEW CLASS OF WINNERS

At the end of the season, the Class-A Southern Association was reclassified as an A1 league. Moore's Crackers welcomed the new classification with a bang. They dominated the '36 season after bolting to a 26–4 start and never looking back before their 94–59 (.614) finish.

The Crackers won with pitching and defense, leading the league in fielding and again enjoying the services of Thomas on the mound. Atlanta even received a special mid-season charge when Brooklyn optioned Dutch Leonard, who went 13–3 after Mann signed him for the Crackers. Leonard's winning percentage of .813 was the best of any tosser that year.

65

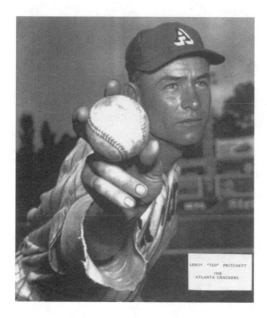

Leroy "Ted" Pritchett
in 1938.

More than 301,000 Atlanta fans enjoyed the Cracker home games in person, while league attendance (1,164,265) was the best since 1927. The Shaughnessy playoffs brought in 115,000 fans throughout the league, even though the Crackers lost three games to two to New Orleans in round one.

In 1937 the Crackers finished third, with a record of 84–66 (.560). Hugh Luby scored the most hits of anyone in the league that year, 208 over 153 games. Atlanta defeated Memphis three games to two in the Shaughnessies' first round, but lost to New Orleans, its 1936 nemesis, over a seven-game set, four games to three.

ROCKING THE SOUTHERN'S NEW HOME

After 19 successful years as Southern Association president, federal judge John D. Martin resigned in 1938 with a full two years left on his contract, citing the pressure of his legal and judicial responsibilities. The league elected Major Trammell Scott of Atlanta as its new presi-

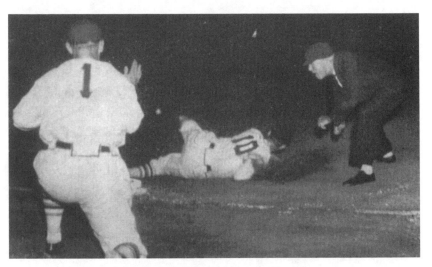

Atlanta's Johnny Hill (10) slides into third base in this night game as manager
Eddie Moore (1) looks on.

dent, and the '38 Crackers welcomed the Southern's new headquar-
ters to Atlanta by dominating the season.

Third baseman Johnny Hill won the batting title with a .332 average.
Paul Richards, later to become Baltimore manager, took over that year
as player/manager, and he kept the helm until 1941. Richards imple-
mented brilliant field tactics throughout the year and hit over .300
himself. Tom "Lefty" Sunkel posted a rare pitcher's triple crown
(21–5, 178K, 2.33 ERA), while righthander Bill Beckman added
prowess from the other side of the mound (20–13).

"Richard's Rifles" spent the year in first place, entitling them to
take on the league's best players in the first-ever Southern Association
All-Star Game. Under the lights at Ponce de Leon they destroyed the
All-Stars, 16–6, won their eighth pennant, roared through the
Shaughnessies undefeated and then whipped Beaumont in
the Dixie Series. The Atlanta Crackers had struck the first
Southern Association grand slam.

67

The next year was something of a letdown, as Atlanta finished a distant fourth with an 83–67 (.553) record. Emil Mailho led the league with 122 runs scored and Russ Peters hit the most triples that year, 15. Pitcher Luman Harris pitched only one ball in an August 5 game against New Orleans yet was credited with a victory. With the bases loaded, a Pelicans batter flied out on the first pitch thrown by Harris to end the inning. The score was tied at the time, end of the first half of the ninth, when Atlanta scored a run in the last half, winning 6–5 for Harris.

The Crackers ended the year by whipping first-place Chattanooga in the first round of the Shaughnessies, but lost to Nashville over a full seven-game set. And as the decade came to an end, Earl Mann was solidifying his reputation as one of the league's most astute baseball men. The 1940s would see the minor leagues' first great golden era, and the Atlanta Crackers would be at the forefront.

The Lookouts' Joe Engel and the Crackers' Earl Mann had a fierce but friendly rivalry as team general managers, and later as team owners.

Joe Engel:
"The Barnum of the Bushes"

Atlanta Crackers executive Earl Mann's primary competitor in the Southern Association came from Chattanooga's team president Joe Engel. Over the years, Mann and he developed a friendly yet fierce competition.

Engel served as president and chief stockholder of the Lookouts from 1929 through 1965, and was known as "the Barnum of the Bushes." When he became president of the Lookouts in 1929, at the age of 36, he did so with the full support of his old friend Clark C. Griffith, owner of the Washington Senators, who had decided to make Chattanooga his top farm club.

Engel's association with the Senators ran deep, for he was a native of the nation's capital and as a boy he hustled off to the ballpark every chance he got. His good fortunes began in 1907, when he was hired as the team's mascot and bat boy, a post he held for three years. In 1911, the Senators signed Engel to a playing contract, but through the years, he never quite lived up to expectations as a world-beater on the mound.

Troubled by wildness, he saw brief service with Cincinnati and Cleveland, and pitched a couple of innings for the Senators again in 1920. Between his sojourns back to the majors, Engel also pitched for Atlanta before finally retiring from active play and going into the game's business side.

Almost immediately afterward, Engel was hired as a super scout for Griffith, and in effect became a one-man scouting team.

The scouting job that brought Engel the most satisfaction was the signing of Joe Cronin in mid-1928. He bought the 21-year-old shortstop from the Kansas City Blues of the American Association for $7,500 without Griffith's approval. When Engel telephoned the Old Fox about the purchase, the conversation was congenial until Engel mentioned the price and the fact that Cronin was hitting a puny .245. Then Griffith hit the ceiling, raging, "He's not my ball player! He's yours! You keep him and don't either you or Cronin show up at the Washington ballpark!"

Griffith relented the next day. "Well, as long as he's mine and I have to pay for him, let me at least have a look at him." Cronin became a hard-hitting, sure-handed shortstop for the Senators, winning the MVP award in 1930 and managing Washington to the American League pennant in 1933.

One of Engel's first acts upon becoming Lookout president was to build a new ballpark which was christened Engel Stadium. It seated 12,000, and soon after the stadium was completed, Engel put in a press room, the first in the league. A great believer in the power of the press, Engel always made it his business to win the friendship of sportswriters and other newsmen. "Without them, where would we be?" he asked.

Engel was one of the most colorful characters in baseball history. His flair for the unexpected and dramatic—and the ridiculous—was rarely matched, even by Earl Mann.

In 1931, Engel's Lookouts became the first team in professional baseball history to sign a female baseball player, 17-year-old Jackie Mitchell, who had been tutored by Cardinals' pitcher Dazzy Vance. In April, she even made an appearance in an exhibition game against the New York Yankees, and legend has it that she struck out Babe Ruth and Lou Gehrig in succession. Several Yankee players even confirmed her account of the story.

In one legendary trade, Engel swapped shortstop Johnny Jones to Charlotte in the South Atlantic League, a team that was also a Washington affiliate, for a 25-pound turkey. Engel then invited Southern Association sportswriters to a turkey dinner. "I still think I got the worst of that deal," Engel would later recall. "That was a mighty tough turkey."

Engel also traded a player to the Pacific Coast League for a case of grapefruit. To attract fans to his games, he once placed hundreds of dollars all over the field and allowed four or five fans to run over the field and pick up as much money as they could in 30 minutes.

Engel and Mann regularly engaged in opening-day attendance contests, the loser of which would receive a bronzed horse's rear end as a trophy. "My dad never won any of those contests," Oreon Mann would recall. "But once he did arrange for a pile of horse manure to be dumped in Engel's front yard."

"I always try to look on the light side of things," Engel once said, "and I live every day just as if it were New Year's Eve."

FIFTH INNING

SHATTERED BARRIERS

"Unless some sort of rule is passed making it impossible to put nine men on the field, baseball is not dead."

—National Baseball Commissioner Kennesaw Mountain Landis, 1941

While World War II enveloped Europe, the Atlanta Crackers and the Southern Association were winning and prospering.

Paul Richards, who was becoming more and more a hot major-league prospect, led the Crackers to a second-place posting in 1940 (93–58, .616), while Emil Mailho led the league in most runs scored, 144 over a 152-game span. Luman Harris, with a 15–9 record, was the Southern's fourth-winningest pitcher. On September 6, while playing the Memphis Chicks, Atlanta's Willard Marshall set an all-time league record for the most putouts by an outfielder over two consecutive games: twelve in 13 innings on September 5 and nine in nine innings the next day.

The following year (the same year in which Delta Air Lines relocated

Tickets from the 1940s.

from a Louisiana bayou to the capital city of the South) would become another milestone for the Atlanta Crackers, a club that Earl Mann would later call his all-time favorite. It would also mark the beginning of a period after which baseball would never be the same.

To start the season, Atlanta won 26 and lost only five of its first 31 contests, in a span from April 10 to May 12, 1941; they went on to win 30 of their first 35 games. On May 30, as Joe DiMaggio was just beginning his hitting streak of 56 straight games in New York, Atlanta clobbered the Knoxville Smokies, 20–0. Two days later, they knocked eight balls out of Sulfur Dell in a win over the Nashville Vols. At the 1941 All-Star game, Atlanta won handily 5–0.

Again managed by Richards, this pennant express included sluggers Burge, Mailho and Marshall, and a magnificent fly-catcher named Buddy Bates, who hit .323 that year. Les Burge, a giant first baseman, set a then-Cracker record of 38 home runs as the Southern's home-run leader and drove in a league-leading 144 runs as RBI champ. Ed Huesser was the team's top pitcher at 20–8 and the league's third-best; he also finished the year with a perfect fielding average. The '41 Crackers led all other teams with a fielding percentage of .971, en route to a first-place 99–55 (.643) finish, 15 and a half games ahead of the Nashville Vols, and a 10th franchise pennant.

But the Atlanta blitzkrieg wasn't enough to hold up during the

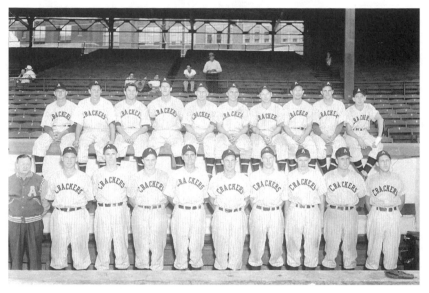

The 1941 Crackers.
Tracey O'Neal Collection, Pullen Library, Georgia State University.

Shaughnessies, as they defeated the Lookouts three games to one in the first round but lost to Nashville over a seven-game set in the finals. The Vols would go on to whip Dallas in the Dixie Series.

Three months later, on December 7, 1941, the Japanese bombed the U.S. Pacific Fleet based at Pearl Harbor, and the entire world changed overnight.

THE YOUNG, THE OLD, AND THE 4-F

Unlike other minor leagues, the Southern Association continued to operate a full schedule throughout World War II.

On January 14, 1942, National Baseball Commissioner Kennesaw Mountain Landis wrote to Franklin D. Roosevelt, asking for some direction. "Baseball is about to adopt schedules, sign players,

75

1939 Atlanta Crackers
replica jersey

make vast commitments, go to training camps. What do you want us to do?" Landis wrote. "If you believe we ought to close down for the duration of the war, we are ready to do so immediately. If you feel we ought to continue, we would be delighted to do so. We await your order."

Roosevelt replied, "I honestly feel it would be best for the country to keep baseball going. There will be fewer people unemployed and everybody will work longer hours and harder than ever before. And that means that they ought to have a chance for recreation and for taking their minds off their work even more than before. . . . As to the players themselves, I know you agree with me that individual players who are of active military or naval age should go, without question, into the services. Even if the actual quality of the teams is lowered by the greater use of older players, this will not dampen the popularity of the sport."

The game's professional leagues were thus given the green light to keep playing.

Landis and Mann knew each other quite well and had developed a good working relationship with each other over the years. Despite the judge's sometimes heavy-handed approach to ruling the game, Mann respected Landis, and that respect was returned. "Whenever Judge Landis would visit Atlanta, my dad would take him over to Kennesaw to see the mountain he was named for," Oreon Mann

76

recalls. (Landis was named for the Battle of Kennesaw Mountain by his father, a Union Army surgeon).

Landis was firm in his faith that the game could be continued with over-age, under-age and 4-F players, both in the majors and minors. The result was a '42 season that was less than scin-tillating for Atlanta.

Richards returned to manage the '42 campaign, leading the team to a 76–78 (.494) record, enough to finish fifth. Worth mentioning is a June 30 game against Knoxville, in which Atlanta's Tommy O'Brien had four assists, the most ever by a Southern Association outfielder. The Little Rock Travelers won the pennant that year with a record of 87–59 (.596).

1939 Atlanta Crackers
replica jacket.

A NEW PRESIDENT IN TROUBLING TIMES

After the '42 season Major Trammell Scott resigned as league president, and Billy Evans, a future Hall of Famer who had been a superb American League umpire from 1906 through 1927 before becoming a major-league executive, was elected president. His main task was to keep the Southern Association up and running while a slew of other minor leagues were shutting down because of wartime travel restrictions and a rapidly declining pool of players. In all, about 3,000 minor league players from across the nation went to war.

Forty-three minor leagues were operating in 1940, drawing a total paid attendance of almost 20 million. But

77

attendance dropped to 16 million the next year as the nation became distracted by the looming crisis overseas.

In 1942 the number of minor leagues dropped to 31. Just 10 minor leagues operated in 1943; that number remained the same in 1944 as Germany and Italy collapsed. The Texas League was one of those circuits that suspended operation in 1943, 1944 and 1945; thus no Dixie Series were played during those years.

Nonetheless, the Southern Association owners and officials, Earl Mann included, were determined to keep the game going and protect their investments, no matter who they had to recruit.

With Richards headed to the big leagues where he belonged, Al Leitz managed the Crackers for the first half of the season, leaving with a record of 36–35 (.507), while Harry Hughes finished out the season at the helm with an unremarkable record of 24–44 (.353). All total, Atlanta finished next to last, while Nashville posted a pennant-winning record of 83–55 (.601).

Mann effected one of his most famous coups in 1944, when he signed all-time Southern Association and major-league star Hazen "Ki Ki" Cuyler as manager. While starring with the Chicago Cubs, Cuyler had carved out a future Hall of Fame career. He managed the Brooklyn Dodgers in 1938 and then the Chattanooga Lookouts in '39, where he led the team to a Southern Association pennant.

It didn't take long for Cuyler to turn the Crackers around, with the help of a talented 19-year-old fresh out of college.

NO SMOKING, DRINKING OR CUSSING

Lloyd Gearhart had suffered from rheumatic fever as a child, which resulted in a slight heart murmur later in life. He also had a trick knee and a perforated ear drum, all of which combined to keep him from being drafted by Uncle Sam. So he turned to baseball.

"I was playing for an A-ball team in Dayton, where my manager was a fellow named Dick Bass," Lloyd Gearhart said. "He and Ki Ki were friends, and when the Crackers recruited me, Dick persuaded me to sign." Gearhart considered it great advice "because Cuyler taught me most of what I know about baseball."

"Cuyler was a great guy and a great manager," Gearhart said. "He was a perfectionist, very meticulous. He was very clean-cut and didn't smoke, drink or swear . . . and he didn't like for his players to, either."

In 1944, the squeaky-clean Crackers finished first with an overall record of 86–53 (.619). Lindsay Deal had the most hits of anyone in the

1947 Atlanta Crackers replica cap.

league that year, 190 over 135 games. Deal also was the RBI champ with 124, and hit 40 doubles, more than anyone else. Outfielder Billy Goodman scored the most runs, 122 in 137 games, and he and Mel Ivy tied for the most triples in the league, 13. On July 4, the Crackers' Marshall Mauldin got six base hits in a game against Memphis.

As the last world war drew to a close, the Atlanta Crackers would be victorious again under Cuyler, posting a record of 94–46 (.671). As a team, they led the league with the best fielding percentage, .965. Ted Cieslak was the Southern's top slugger, scoring 127 runs in 140 games; Cieslak was also the RBI champ with 120, stats impressive enough to make him the Southern Association MVP in 1945.

The Crackers dominated the league on the mound as well. Only six pitchers in the history of the Southern Association finished with a winning percentage of better than .900, and of those six, only one has been a 20-game winner: a rangy Cracker righthander named Lew Carpenter. A highly consistent winner during '45, Carpenter finished with 22 wins

◇

against two defeats for a percentage of .917. In addition, he won a game in the Shaughnessy playoffs for which he received no credit in his final winning percentage.

Another truly remarkable feature of Carpenter's miracle year was the fact that the 1945 season was two weeks old before he made his first start. Thus, he compiled his 22–2 record in about four months of actual pitching.

Carpenter won his first start on May 11, 1945, and then was beaten by Memphis in a ninth-inning rally, when wildness and one bad play gave the Chicks enough runs to win. This hard-luck loss was followed by seven consecutive wins before Chattanooga decisively trimmed Carpenter 8–3 on June 29. Following was 15 wins in a row, topped off by a victory over New Orleans in the Shaughnessies that does not appear in the official yearly record.

THE CAPITAL OF THE MINORS

With the end of the war, the Southern Association enjoyed a boom period, as did most of professional baseball. 1946 was a banner year at the gate as the league drew 1,831,236 fans, which far surpassed the previous high of 1,351,570 in 1925. Atlanta rolled up the highest attendance of any association team in history by drawing 395,699 fans, breaking its own season's record of 330,795 set in 1935.

Instead of attendance dropping off after such a mark, the reverse happened in 1947. Attendance records went right through the ceiling as the total reached 2,180,344. Two clubs reached the 400,000 figure: the Crackers—with a league-leading 404,584—and New Orleans, with 400,036.

This was the height of minor league baseball in the United States. A total of 464 teams in 59 leagues drew 42 million fans. And Atlanta was the game's capital.

By then the Sunday afternoon doubleheader had become a Southern Association trademark, but it hadn't always been the case. Local pastor Dr. Louis Newton was firmly against playing baseball on Sunday. So for years Mann followed a policy that the games wouldn't start until after folks had a chance to return home from their weekly holy gatherings. But after World War II, as baseball and Cracker-mania took the city by storm year by year, Mann's early-starting Sunday afternoon double-headers would become a ritual.

The Crackers opened their 1946 training camp in Gainesville, Fla., two weeks earlier than usual; Cuyler was unsure what kind of playing shape his men would be in after years of jumping in foxholes and dodging the fascists' bullets. (The Crackers contributed 75 men to the war; five never came home. They were J.W. "Duck" McKee, Frank Haggerty, Troy Furr, James Stewart and Milton Rosenstein.)

"FIGHTING FOR DEAR LIFE"

That year, the Crackers had so many former and brand-new players in training camp that Cuyler set up four teams of prospects that would play against each other in intramural games; two would play in the morning, and two in the afternoon.

"The boys will be fighting for dear life, not only to win games but to prevent very able substitutes from taking their jobs away from them," Cuyler said. "But we don't want to overlook any good men who are wild now, but merely need a little seasoning in order to settle them down into steady players."

That year also saw the Southern Association newly classified as a AA league, and Cuyler led the team to a 12th pennant (96–58, .623). Outfield Billy Goodman (whom Mann would later sell to Boston for $35,000) hit .387 and Cieslak, on his way to a second straight league MVP award, hit .352. On the mound, Ayers was 23–10, had the lowest ERA in the league (1.95) and was the association's winningest pitcher. Other outstanding Crackers on the mound were Earl McGowan (22–10) and Shelby Kinney (20–9). Gearhart, playing every game on the schedule, led the league with 139 runs scored.

On June 12, the second all-time highest score in a Southern Association game was set: Atlanta 23, Nashville 20. A total of 43 hits were scored in the game. On July 28, 1946, Ralph Ellis batted in nine runs, while Cieslak scored six base hits against Little Rock later in the year. In the Shaughnessies, Atlanta defeated New Orleans four games to three, then faced Memphis, who had beaten Chattanooga four games to one. Atlanta whipped Memphis four games to three in the finals, but was swept in four by Dallas in the '46 Dixie Series.

MANN'S FINALLY THE MAN

In 1947 Earl Mann formally bought the Crackers from the Coca-Cola Co. for close to $500,000. At that time the owner of the New York Giants, Horace Stoneham, had made an offer to Coke CEO Robert Woodruff to not only buy the team but also some Coke property. Hughes Spalding was aware of Mann's desire to own the Crackers outright, and suggested waiting to see how much of an offer Mann could develop. Mann, along with Hal Aronson, an influential and prosperous wholesale liquor distributor, made a $449,000 offer to buy the team from Coke; Aronson signed the note and C&S Bank provided the funds.

One of his first acts as owner was to sell Gearhart's contract to the New York Giants for $75,000. "Earl Mann was one of the most generous men I've ever met," Gearhart said. "I signed for nothing, but he still gave me a little bonus. My three straight years in Atlanta were beautiful."

1952

Ralph "Country" Brown

Shown in his final season, Ralph "Country" Brown played
for the Crackers from 1948–52.

Mann soon signed a farm boy from northwest Georgia. Ralph
"Country" Brown would make the park's outfield his own personal
territory.

Brown came to Atlanta after his minor-league career stalled in the
New York Yankees organization, where he had signed fresh out of
the Air Force. While playing at Daniel Field in Augusta, Ga., teammate Dutch Lumberger christened Brown with his soon-to-
be-famous nickname.

83

"Dutch came up to me one day and said, 'Boy, where you from?' And I told him I was from Summerville, Ga. And he said, 'I've never heard of that. That must be way out in the country.' And the name just stuck," Brown recalled.

After winning consecutive batting titles and league MVP awards with the Class-C Tampa Smokers and AA Augusta Tigers, Brown spent a little time at AAA Newark, only to be told that he would be demoted to Class A and switched to first base, because his arm was too weak. At age 26, he went home to Summerville in hopes of being traded. Ten days later, Mann heard he was available and purchased his contract. Brown's salary was $500 a month, and he was destined to become one of Atlanta's most popular, beloved players.

Country's first year as a Cracker was in 1947, a season in which Atlanta would come in fifth (73–78, .483) and yet still lead the league in attendance (404,584 for Atlanta, 2,180,344 for the entire league).

The Crackers, who already held the record for the longest day game ever played in the Southern Association, set the record for the longest night game on August 8, 1947, against the Bears in Mobile. The game went 21 innings and ended in a 4–4 tie. Mobile scored four runs in the third inning but was through scoring for the night. The Bears' George Shuba accounted for three of the runs by hitting a three-run round tripper. In the fourth, Atlanta's Babe Ellis homered with two on, and in the sixth Ellis again drove in the tying run with a single. Bill Ayers went the full game for Atlanta on the mound.

Despite the previous year's disappointing finish, the largest opening-day crowd in Southern Association history greeted the Crackers at Poncey in 1948, when 21,812 turned out to see them play the Birmingham Barons. Ki Ki Cuyler's last year in Atlanta ended with a sixth-place finish (69–85, .448). Pitcher Shelby Kinney had a perfect fielding average.

Another memorable event that year came in mid-season, when Mann made the only trade of its kind in baseball history.

AN ANNOUNCER FOR A CATCHER

Before the Japanese wake-up call at Pearl Harbor, Ernie Harwell had been serving as sports director at Atlanta's WSB-AM, one of the Southeast's most powerful radio stations. Then the Marines called in 1942, and off went Harwell into the armed forces.

On a visit back to Atlanta in 1943, however, Mann asked him to call a few games on radio, which he did. "But the Marines didn't like that too much, even though I gave all my paychecks to the Red Cross," Harwell said. "Earl told me to come back after my tour was over, and he'd make me the regular announcer for all of the Cracker games."

So, in 1946, Harwell returned. At the time, WATL-AM had taken over the broadcast rights to the Cracker games, and wanted sports director Stan Raymond to be the announcer. "Earl really went to bat for me, because he had promised me the job," Harwell recalled. "When the '46 opening day rolled around, the station still hadn't made a decision. But around the middle of that morning, Earl called me and said 'We licked 'em. Come on down.'

"That kind of loyalty is something you don't forget."

Harwell called Cracker games until 1948. "A lot of our programming came from the Mutual Radio Network," he said. "There were some games that we'd join in the middle of the second or third inning, or even later, until the Mutual programs were over."

Road games were recreated in WATL's studio, which was in the basement of the Georgian Terrace Hotel across the street from the Fox Theater. "A telegrapher from Western Union would feed me the information from Birmingham, Chattanooga or wherever, and I'd recreate the action from the wires," he said. "I also had photos of all the league stadiums, and would refer to certain points of interest at the park in my broadcasts."

In the middle of the '48 season, however, the legendary Red Barber became seriously ill. The Brooklyn Dodgers' announcer was hospitalized for a severe stomach ulcer, and Dodger owner Branch Rickey needed an announcer badly. "Rickey called Earl, and said he'd like for me to become the Dodger announcer," Harwell said. "Earl said that even though I was under contract to the Crackers, he'd trade me for Cliff Dapper, a catcher for the Dodgers' Montreal Triple-A team." This marked the first and only time in baseball history that an announcer was swapped for a player.

The next year Dapper was promoted to player/manager of the Crackers, and led them to a fifth-place (71–82, .464) standing. Country Brown stole 33 bases that year, the most of anyone in the league. On August 19, Dapper had an unassisted double play against the Pelicans, and over Sept. 9–11, the Crackers and Barons set a Southern Association record for the fastest five games in one series. The first contest lasted 1:14 (nine innings), while the others lasted 1:55, 1:48 and 1:17 (nine innings each) and 1:10 over a final, seven-inning game that was called on account of rain.

In 1949 Mann made a slight adjustment to Poncey's dimensions. To cut the considerable blast required to hit a home run over leftfield, fences were constructed and a short hedge was planted straight from the leftfield line to near the magnolia tree in deep right center. Since the hedge was only two feet high, many players caught fly balls only to fall over the other side of the hedge, which resulted in a ground-rule homer.

Gearhart returned in 1949 and was paired in the outfield with Brown in right and Goodman in left. "I chased a few balls up that outfield bank," Gearhart said. "I was able to catch a lot of fly balls that were hit farther than 450 feet. I actually hit three balls in one '49 game that were over 450 feet in distance and were still caught by the opposing outfielders." He also hit two into the leftfield bleachers.

"WE NEVER HEARD FROM THE GRAND DRAGON AGAIN"

Despite the popularity of the game of baseball, blacks and whites still played the game separately in the 1940s. That is, until a certain even-tempered young man from south Georgia smashed the color line with the help of a teetotaling, rabidly anti-Communist—and courageous—baseball executive.

Jackie Robinson was born in 1919 to a family of sharecroppers in Cairo, Ga., but his family moved to Pasadena, Calif., when he was just a baby. He attended UCLA, and was the leading football rusher for the Bruins in 1939. He also was the conference's top basketball scorer and record-breaking long jumper; this four-letter star actually put up his poorest statistics in baseball.

After college, he became a lieutenant in the U.S. Army, and won acquittal in a court martial for refusing to sit at the back of a military bus. After his tour of duty, he joined the Kansas City Monarchs, hitting .387 in 1945. Dodgers scout Clyde Sukeforth reported back to his boss in Brooklyn that "the more you talked to the guy, the more you were impressed. . . . The determination was written all over him." Robinson was educated, a solid player and even-keeled—just the type of man Branch Rickey was looking for.

In 1946, Robinson signed with the Dodgers to play second for the team's Montreal Royals AAA club. The next year, Rickey traded Dodger second baseman Eddie Starky to the Boston Braves for first baseman Ray Sanders, thus making room for the first black man ever to play in major-league baseball.

The Brooklyn Dodgers played the Crackers in a three-game exhibition series at Poncey in 1949. Jackie Robinson's participation made it the first integrated professional sporting event in Atlanta.

Tracey O'Neal Collection, Pullen Library, Georgia State University.

Two years later, Mann arranged for a three-game exhibition series with the Dodgers at Poncey. The Dodgers came through Atlanta with Robinson, Roy Campanella, Pee Wee Reese, Duke Snyder, Carl Fenilla and Gil Hodges.

If the games came off, it would mark the first time that blacks and whites would compete against each other in Atlanta in a professional, organized sporting event. The Ku Klux Klan, though, was determined that the contests would never be played.

"The Klan's Grand Dragon called Dad, threatening him if Robinson played here," said Oreon Mann. "My father rarely ever got angry, but, Lord, when he did. . . . Well, after telling this Grand Dragon where to go, he called [then-police chief] Herbert Jenkins.

"The Klan called again later at the park, and Jenkins happened to be standing there when the call came in. Dad told the Grand Dragon that he was going to put Jenkins on the line, and told him to repeat his threats to the Atlanta police chief.

"We never heard from that Grand Dragon again."

The games came off without a hitch, and the final game on April 10, 1949, drew an all-time Poncey crowd of 25,221, including 13,885 black fans. The Crackers would win one of the three games by a score of 8–4.

"What I remember most about those games was the tremendous number of people who came," Gearhart recalled. "What Robinson did in his career was a tremendously dangerous thing to do. Back in those days, it was really rough. But the games came off with no trouble at all."

That year, 1949, was the best the minors had ever seen, with 59 leagues, 7,800 players and 20 million fans paying their hard-earned money to see them. But many challenges remained, and the example set by Jackie Robinson would lead another player in the 1950s to crumble yet another racial barrier, a man who would walk a more difficult, yet far less heralded, road.

FAIR BALL!!

THOSE WE REMEMBER

"In 43 years of sportswriting that was the most fun I've ever had."

—Jesse Outlar

From 1950 until 1957, when he became sports editor of the *Atlanta Constitution*, Jesse Outlar traveled with and wrote about the greatest Cracker teams of all time.

Atlanta in the 1950s was becoming a metropolis. The skyline was changing, and under the leadership of dynamic political and business leaders like William Hartsfield, Mills Lane and Robert Woodruff, Atlanta was crashing through the boundary that separates drowsy, down-sized provincial villages from bustling, hyperactive cities that never sleep.

As the 1950s dawned, the Crackers were reaping the fruits of their past success. "Ponce Park was great," Outlar said. "Earl Mann ran a major league operation in the minors. Engel Stadium in Chattanooga and Rickwood Field in Birmingham were among the better parks, but Atlanta was the best.

◇

"There was very little violent crime. After the game, me and the Western Union telegraph guy were often the only ones left, and no one ever bothered us. The most relaxed place in the world was at Ponce de Leon Ball Park."

THE LAST OF THE INDEPENDENTS

By the 1950s, many minor-league teams across the nation had signed working agreements with major-league clubs, mainly because it made good economic sense. An independent operator was responsible for all of his team's expenses. But once a major-league club agreed to field their prospects at one of the lower classifications, the major-league club would assume the player's salaries, relieving a substantial financial burden from the major-league operator.

In 1950—the 50th Southern Association season—the Crackers, the last independent team in the league, signed a working agreement with the Braves, giving Boston the right to farm its players to the Crackers' Class-AA franchise while retaining the athletes' contracts. As a result, some of the game's best players would come through Poncey on their way to the big show, including the only Atlanta Cracker other than Luke Appling to make it to Cooperstown.

Born Oct. 13, 1931, in Texarkana, Texas, and then growing up in Santa Barbara, Calif., Eddie Mathews signed with the Boston Braves in 1949, after graduating from high school. He joined the Crackers in 1950 at age 18, and he immediately began making a name for himself. On the field, he displayed the kind of power that would lead him to blast 512 balls out of major-league parks. In addition to being "the best drag bunter there ever was," according to U.S. senator and baseball afficionado Zell Miller, Mathews' swat was one of only "three or four perfect swings [secn] in my time," according to Ty Cobb. Off the field, that same physical prowess kept people from getting in his face.

Hall of Famer Eddie Mathews began his baseball career with the Crackers and was the only player to wear a Braves uniform in Boston, Milwaukee and Atlanta. He and teammate Hank Aaron formed the greatest home-run hitting duo ever. Mathews hit 512 and Aaron hit 755—60 more than Babe Ruth and Lou Gehrig.
National Baseball Hall of Fame Library

BASEBALL'S HEAVYWEIGHT CHAMP

"I've always contended that Eddie Mathews could have been a heavyweight boxer," Outlar said. "He was undefeated in fights, both on the field and off."

"Take my word for it, he could have been heavyweight champion," said Ellis Clary, Cracker second baseman in 1950 and one of the most colorful men ever to wear the uniform. "He had a perfect build, huge forearms. He was a great guy when he was on your side, but if you ever crossed him, there'd be hell to pay."

93

Photographer Bill Wilson shot this 1950 pre-game photo with the promise that the *Atlanta Constitution* would run it only as an above-the-waist shot. *(Left to right)* Ralph "Country" Brown, Hank Eastman, Ebba St. Claire and Eddie Mathews.
Atlanta History Center

Sometimes Mathews didn't even have to fight—his mere presence was enough to break up a brawl. During a 1950 Labor Day game in Birmingham, Clary got into a fracas with the Barons' first baseman, Bob DiPittio, who'd been an amateur boxer in the U.S. Navy. "That was probably the only fight I've ever won," Clary said. "I knocked some of his teeth out." Both Clary and DiPittio were thrown out of the game.

It wasn't long before DiPittio and an extremely large Baron came looking for Clary. What they forgot is that someone standing along the first- or third-base line could look directly past the dugout and into the team's dressing room. In this case, that someone happened to be Eddie Mathews.

"I was taking off my shoes when I heard someone come into our dressing room and roaring like a goddamned lion," Clary remembered. "DiPittio and this other guy were yelling and screaming, and DiPittio was pulling up his lip, showing me where some of his teeth used to be and pointing to them."

By this time, Mathews had seen what was going on and called time. He ran into the dressing room, "cussing out both of 'em and telling them to get the hell out of there," Clary said. "They accommodated his request in a hurry."

Ralph "Country" Brown saw Mathews hit one out of Russwood Park in Memphis. "The Chicks' pitcher, Gus Cariasakis, threw a fastball at Eddie's waist, and my God,

One of the toughest to play the game, Ellis Clary wears his St. Louis Browns uniform, circa 1943–45. Clary enjoyed a 32-year career as a major league scout and is a member of the Georgia Sports Hall of Fame.

he hit that ball incredibly hard," said Brown. "I was on first, and I started my baserunning."

Russwood's outfield signs were 425 feet from home plate. The backstop signs were 20 feet high, and the Memphis Steam Laundry smokestacks were 10 feet beyond that. "That ball went over the backfield fence and over the signs, and hit those stacks 30 or 40 feet from the ground," Brown said. "I stopped running to look at the ball, and when I reached the dugout, (Manager Fred "Dixie") Walker jumps all over me, yelling, 'Don't ever let me see you stop your base running like that again!'

"When he stopped yelling, I said, 'If I ever see a ball hit that hard again, I'm going to stop at look at it again, because that's something you just don't see everyday.'

"Eddie was so strong. He and (Cracker catcher) Ebba St. Claire (who drove in six runs against the Pelicans on May 18, 1950) once got into a fight in the clubhouse. Ebba weighed about 230 and Eddie literally pressed him over his head."

96

OF BASES AND BRAWLS

Brown also was in the middle of the worst brawl ever to break out at Ponce Park, right along with Mathews. It happened during the thick of the 1950 pennant race, when the Crackers hosted Mobile on a Sunday afternoon, the Bears being a half-game behind them in the standings.

Bear hurler Chuck Eisenmann, known throughout the league for his excellent control, thought Cracker pitching coach Whitlow Wyatt was calling his pitches to the Cracker batters—which, 45 years later, Wyatt admitted he was. Eisenmann, feeling the need to take some revenge, hit the Crackers' Rusty Morgan.

"He pitched around our next batter," Brown said. "I was up next, and he hit me in the back. I knew it was intentional, so as I was on my way to first, I told him that either we'll play this game properly or we'll have a goddamned free-for-all. My next time up, the first pitch went right at my head. My cap went one way, my bat went the other, and I hit the dirt." The second pitch was about four feet outside, but Brown swung at it anyway, and then threw the bat at Eisenmann.

"Whitlow was coaching first base, and he picked up the bat and yelled at the pitcher, 'I've got a good mind to throw it at you!'"

That's when all hell broke loose. Both benches emptied, Mathews was tearing at every Mobile cap he could find, and Wyatt—who had come to the game straight from church where he had led the congregation in prayer—had Eisenmann around the neck. "It was the most awful sight you've ever seen," Brown said. "Whitlow was about to kill that pitcher. It took three policemen to get him off."

Incredibly, order was eventually restored and no one was ejected. "But that cured the throwing at batters," Brown said.

The next day, Brown was riding a packed Atlanta Coach Co. bus from downtown to the Ponce de Leon Hotel, where he stayed, and the bus was abuzz with talk of the fight. His fellow riders, who didn't recognize him in his street clothes, asked him if he'd been at the game.

"They were really up in the air about it," he said. "They said to be sure to go to the game that night. I got off the bus and never gave away who I was."

PLANES, BUSES, AND CATTLE CARS

Life as a Cracker in the 1950s was a life on the run. The only time the team used a bus was to head to Birmingham or Chattanooga; otherwise, they traveled by rail, in "cattle cars," as the players called them.

"A lot of times the air conditioning was out and it'd be brutal," Brown said. "There were no travel days; we'd only have four or five days off a year. You'd catch the train right after the game, travel all night, and not get to Little Rock until 10 or 12 the next morning."

"Some of the trains weren't air conditioned," Outlar said. "And during the summer, with those Sunday-afternoon doubleheaders, New Orleans was the worst, with all that humidity."

Outlar recalls during one road trip, on an old Pullman train car, Clary turned to Cracker team secretary Jasper Donaldson and said, "This Pullman is so damn old, the hair on the upholstery has turned gray."

"You had to be a tough S.O.B. to play every day during the week and stand out there in Poncey at 1:30 in the afternoon for a Sunday doubleheader," Clary said.

"It was a job just carrying those flannel uniforms around," said Bob Montag, who joined the Crackers in 1954. "Come July and August, those bats got a little heavy too. But we were there to play baseball, not complain about the conditions. Sure, we didn't smell too good, but what the hell did we care?"

98

A GREAT WAY TO START THE DECADE

Besides serving as manager, Fred "Dixie" Walker, a longtime Dodger star, played rightfield until mid-season 1950, when he finally retired for good. With Mathews' 32 homers, .363 average and 106 RBIs, and a hard-living, hard-throwing right-handed rock named Art Fowler winning 19 games on the mound, Atlanta won the '50 championship.

Ben Thorpe, a top Southern Association outfielder when at Little Rock and still a force in 1950, led Atlanta at the bat—despite having a broken jaw—with a .324 average. He also recorded 195 hits.

Shortstop Gene Verble led the league in most runs scored, 118. Pitcher Andrew Elko, over a 50-game career spread, had a perfect fielding average, while Dick Hoover was the league's fourth-winningest pitcher, posting a 16–7 record and 3.35 ERA. During the

Raising the 1950 Southern Association pennant at Ponce de Leon Ball Park.
Tracey O'Neal Collection, Pullen Library, Georgia State University.

Southern All-Star Game, Atlanta clobbered the league's best players, 8–2. Wyatt, worried about overworking the pitching staff, threw four innings in front of the fourth-largest crowd ever to see a Southern Association All-Star game: 15,293 strong at Poncey.

But the team faltered during the playoffs, mainly because Mathews had become very ill. "He couldn't see straight because of all that penicillin he was taking," Clary said. "That's probably the only thing that kept us from going all the way."

"THE GREATEST GAME EVER"
And Clary himself went no farther with the Crackers than the '50 season. He headed to Chattanooga, after which he began a remarkable scouting and managerial career.

◇

His baseball experience began in 1935 in the Georgia-Florida League, and nine years later he was a part of the World Series St. Louis Browns team. He came to Atlanta via the Baltimore Orioles of the International League. "In the Southern Association, we were there because we wanted to play baseball," Clary said. "We had a great league that was made up of more mature players than you find in the minors today. And the quality of play was good; every team drew large crowds wherever they were."

Fred "Dixie" Walker starred with the Brooklyn Dodgers for nine seasons before joining the Crackers as manager.
Tracey O'Neal Collection, Pullen Library, Georgia State University.

Over his 59 years in baseball, Clary played, coached, managed and scouted in every level of professional organized baseball, including for the Minnesota Twins, Washington Senators, Toronto Blue Jays and Chicago White Sox of the majors. And while the quality of the game may be in some ways better today than it was in his prime, Clary has nothing but disdain for today's unionized players and their leadership.

"Baseball was the greatest game ever devised by the human mind, until the players started listening to their union leaders," he said. "The players who stand in front of the television cameras and say they're looking out for the game's future are telling the biggest lie that's ever

After a stint with the Crackers, Chuck Tanner played for the Braves, Cubs, Indians and Angels from 1955–62, batting .261 with 21 homers and 105 RBIs. He managed the White Sox (1970–75), Oakland Athletics (1976), Pirates (1977–85) and Braves (1986–88). *Tracy O'Neal, National Baseball Hall of Fame Library*

been told. We're the ones who laid the game's foundation, but today's players don't want to hear that."

TWO IN A ROW?

By the time spring training was over in 1951, the Crackers were looking like a pretty good bet for another consecutive pennant. Instead, they finished an awful sixth, with a 76–78 record (.494), in part because 19-year-old Mathews had joined the U.S. Navy and missed half of the season. The only reason he rejoined the team at all was because he was discharged after his father was diagnosed with tuberculosis.

While the season was a tremendous disappointment, several individual performances stood out. Jack Dittmer led the league in doubles with 42. Don Liddle, with a 14–6 record and a 2.92 ERA, was the fourth-highest-rated pitcher in the league.

And 1951 saw the arrival of a future World Series-winning manager. Chuck Tanner hit Atlanta straight out of Owensboro, Ky., home of the Oilers, and he'd stick around until the '54 season was over. From there, he played with the Milwaukee Braves until

1957, then with the Cubs, Indians and Angels. After that, a minor-league managerial career led him to the Sister Sledge-soundtracked "We Are Family" days of the 1979 World Series-winning Pittsburgh Pirates.

"Ponce de Leon was the big leagues to me," Tanner said. "I wanted to play baseball so much I would have gone out there and played in a burlap sack. The Southern Association was just like playing in the majors. And if you were hurt or weren't healthy, you got out there and played anyway because if you didn't, someone else was ready to take your place, and you'd never get your spot back."

In 1953, Mathews was called up by the Braves for their last year in Boston. After the team moved to Milwaukee, he, along with a particularly famous teammate by the name of Aaron, provided one of the most potent one-two offensive punches in baseball history. From 1954–66, they combined for 863 homers, the highest total for teammates in major league history. Mathews was one of only five players to hit an extra-inning, game-ending home run in the World Series, and was the only man to play for the Braves in Boston, Milwaukee and Atlanta. He was also on the cover of the premiere issue of *Sports Illustrated,* August 16, 1954. Mathews' baseball career ended in 1974 in the same city where it began, Atlanta, as manager of the Braves. He died February 17, 2001, at the age of 69.

AN ICON FOR A WHOLE WAY OF LIFE

Tanner quickly got to know his opponents, one in particular. "Ellis Clary was one tough son of a gun. If you played in the Southern Association in those days, you knew that he would spike you. You'd slide into second, and he'd jump up like he was trying to catch the ball, and come down on your legs with his spikes.

"He'd do anything to win a game. He was playing for the Lookouts when I started, and I still have the cleat marks on my legs where he spiked me during a game, and then he laughed about it later."

The Crackers would finish in second place in 1952, 10 games over .500. Walker still was captaining the ship and, for some reason, Dixie and Country never got along. "He even suspended me once and never even told me why," Brown said. Finally, during a '52 road trip to Birmingham, Walker dropped a bombshell.

"Before a game against the Barons, Dixie walked over and said he had a hot story, that he'd traded Brown to Chattanooga," *Constitution* reporter Outlar remembered. "At that time, Country Brown was the city's baseball idol. He had a poor arm, but he could fly. He could run faster than anyone I've ever seen."

When Brown was traded, Oreon Mann remembers asking his father, "Is he really gone? When will he be back?"

The answers were "yes, he is" and "never." Country finally retired in 1957 after his poor vision caused him to lose sight of fly balls and an injured right knee ached more and more. He returned to his hometown of Summerville, in northwest Georgia, and eventually took a job in law enforcement. He passed away in 1997.

"Country Brown stood for a whole way of life," the *Atlanta Journal*'s Paul Hemphill wrote during a 1967 Old-Timers Game. "He was a Southern farm boy who had to make his own way. He did not look like a great ballplayer, but he darned near was. . . . He never played in the big leagues, but he hit five of the eight cities in the Southern Association and they loved him everywhere he went because he had this easy, honest flair about him and he was a winner."

"I was fortunate enough to be real fast and could play defense," Brown said. "Any ball I could get to, I'd catch. And I stole a lot of bases." He also stole plenty of time to sign autographs for kids—and didn't charge a penny for any of them.

103

A HUMBLE OLD DODGER

By the end of the '52 season (the same year in which future New York governor Mario Cuomo hit .244 for the Brunswick Pirates in the Georgia-Florida League), the Crackers were heading for a second-place finish. Pitcher Joe Reardon had a perfect fielding average over 36 career games, while Jack Brittin led the team on the mound with a 14–6 record and a 3.60 ERA.

Walker departed after the season, and in came Gene Mauch, who would guide the team to a third-place record in 1953 at 84–70 (.545). William Sinvoic was the Southern's RBI champ with 126. Pitcher Bob Giggie had a perfect fielding average over 38 career games, while Art Fowler was the team's top pitcher, fielding an 18–10 record with a 3.60 ERA.

Mauch had taken a break in his playing career to manage the '53 team, having spent '50 and '51 with the Boston Braves, and then with St. Louis in 1952. But after the '53 season, Boston offered the 28-year-old a chance to resume his athletic career, and Mann was left high and dry without a manager. So he asked a humble, modest old Brooklyn Dodger to take the reins, a man, when interviewed for this book, still said he never was really up to the task.

Hall of Famer and one-time manager for the Dodgers, Giants, Cubs, and Astros Leo Durocher once said that if he had to win one game

104

Atlanta's Beaudry Ford, which sold its first Model T in 1916 and closed its doors in 2001, sponsored this contest night in 1952.

with one pitcher, that thrower would be John Whitlow Wyatt Sr. Wyatt finished up at Cedartown (Ga.) High in 1927, living for football and not caring a flip about baseball. Georgia Tech had even offered him a scholarship to play fullback for the Yellow Jackets.

"This scout from the Detroit Tigers, Eddie Goosetree, had come to scout our school's lefthanded pitcher, Frank Chilton," Wyatt remembered. "Goosetree had given a small boy hanging around the school a $5 bill, and told him to go into town and buy a baseball. The boy came back and said there weren't any $5 baseballs at the store, only those that cost $2.50. So Goosetree sent the boy back into town to buy a couple of those.

"A buddy of mine and I asked that baseball scout to let us play catch with one of those new balls. So we went off to the side of the school, and Goosetree took one look at me and signed me up instead of Lefty Chilton." Indeed, Goosetree was so impressed with the young Wyatt that he even offered to pay the youngster's tuition at Tech if he would agree not to play football.

A COUNTRY BOY GONE TO TOWN

After two months at Tech, Wyatt quit to begin his baseball career. In 1927, the Tigers called Wyatt up to Detroit. "Talk about a country boy goin' to town! I guess my fastball was about 95, though we didn't know how to clock it back then." The Georgia farm boy signed a $3,000 contract.

The Yankees and Babe Ruth came through; Wyatt was throwing batting practice at the time. "Ruth was the type who joked and joked with everyone about anything. When he'd strike out, the fans would boo him terribly. He'd just turn around, tip his cap and bow."

Wyatt played in Evansville, Ind., in 1927 (14–12) and 1928 (22–6). In 1929, he was called up to the big show, the beginning of an unfortunate string of bad luck. He was used only occasionally by Detroit (1929–33); the Chicago White Sox (1933–36); and Cleveland (1937). In 1931, he was sent down temporarily to play with the Beaumont (Texas) Pirates "where the owners thought the warm weather would be better for my arm," he said. In the Texas League, Wyatt pitched against Dizzy Dean and his Houston Buffs team.

"My career was going backward, so I bought 1,400 acres in Buchanan, Ga., and was going to take up farming," Wyatt said. "But in 1938 Milwaukee invited me to their spring training camp, and offered me a contract that promised me $40,000 if I was sold to the majors. I thought that was the most foolish notion I'd ever heard." That year, he developed a slider and a curve to go along with this fastball. He went 24–6 that year, led the league in strikeouts and was named the MVP of the American Association. He knew he'd become a pitcher.

Wyatt's contract was sold to the Dodgers for $30,000, and the next year, despite spending 42 days in the hospital with a shattered kneecap, he won eight straight games, four of them shutouts, and finished with a 2.31 ERA. In 1941 he went 22–10, and pitched the 5–0 pennant-winning game against the Boston Braves. He pitched the second game of the World Series against the Yankees, winning 3–2, as well as the fifth, losing 3–1. The 3–2 victory was the first loss for the Yankees in 11 straight Word Series games.

"I knocked down Joe DiMaggio twice during that game," Wyatt recalled. "The second time, his bat went off into the air, and his cap went flying. On the next pitch, he hit a long fly ball to centerfield. On his way back to the dugout, he said something to me and then I said something to him, and we got into a fight. Afterward, I had to go into the Yankee clubhouse to tell the equipment manager where to send my gear, because I was scheduled to go back to Buchanan after the game. I walked in, and there stood DiMaggio. He said I pitched a helluva game, and deserved to win."

In 1942 Wyatt won 19 games; the next year, 14. He was injured again in '44 and finished 2–6. He spent the next year with the Phillies and then retured to his Buchanan farm, selling insurance and farming for a living. His record as a pitcher was 106–95.

"In 1950, Dixie Walker asked me to be his pitching coach. Then after Mauch left, Earl Mann asked me if I wanted the job," explained Wyatt. "I didn't know if I could manage 20 players, but I needed the money so badly, because I'd missed the players' new pension plan by one year."

So with Whit Wyatt as manager, the Atlanta Crackers were set to make minor-league baseball's most astonishing championship run. And thanks to the courage of Earl Mann, the team started setting records even before the season of '54 began.

THE SOUTH'S JACKIE ROBINSON

"At first, I thought the contract was a joke. I sent the thing back, and then two weeks later I received another one. I called the Braves' home office in Milwaukee, and they said the contract was real.

"I never understood why Atlanta wanted me. We had other black players in the farm system who were better than me. But when I signed, Earl Mann said that my job would be harder than Jackie Robinson's, because I'd have to play in the South."

Integrating the tradition-rich Southern Association was to be the task of Nathaniel Peeples, all the while turning the other cheek in Robinson-esque fashion. Peeples would become the only black man to ever play in the Southern Association, and he did so in 1954 for one of the best Atlanta Cracker teams ever. Earl Mann thought the league was ready for a black player. But Earl Mann, for once, was wrong.

Peeples' career began in 1948 when the strapping six-foot, two-inch, 180-pounder dropped out of LeMoyne College to play catcher for his hometown Memphis Red Sox. In '49, he

107

◇

Crackers catcher Nathaniel "Nat" Peeples played with the Memphis Red Sox and the Kansas City Monarchs before becoming the only African-American ever to play on a Southern Association team, signing with the Atlanta Crackers in 1954.
Atlanta Journal-Constitution

signed with the Kansas City Monarchs, and caught for the legendary ageless wonder himself, Satchel Paige. "He used to call me School Boy, 'cause I was just out of school," Peeples said. "He had tremendous control of the ball. I never saw another player with Satchel's ball control."

108

It was about this time that Peeples met James Thomas Bell—"Cool Papa" by his more famous name. Bell was manager of the Traveling Monarchs and, according to Peeples, "he was everything he's ever been said to be—and probably more." Peeples and the Monarchs played all the great teams of the Negro American League: the Chicago-American Giants, Birmingham Black Barons, Cleveland Buckeyes, the Homestead Grays.

During the 1950 season, Peeples moved on to the Indianapolis Clowns, where he met a teenage Henry Aaron who was "just beginning to show that he could hit it longer and farther than anyone else," Peeples said. The next year, the catcher was sold to the Brooklyn

Dodgers, who already had a promising second-string game-caller behind the plate named Roy Campanella. "That's when I was moved to the outfield, and played in the Dodgers farm system in Elmira and Santa Barbara." Two years later, the Braves picked up Peeples' contract. He played in Evansville, Ind., and then in Pueblo, Colo., when Mann sent him a Crackers' contract.

Only a year earlier, however, Mann had expressed some serious doubts about whether the Southern Association was ready to play blacks and whites. So what changed his mind? Perhaps the success of Henry Aaron at Class-A Jacksonville, where he led the South Atlantic League in runs, hits, RBIs and batting (.362). Players such as Aaron, Felix Mantilla and Horace Garner were setting the minors on fire, despite the vicious, never-ending verbal brutality they received on a circuit of Macon, Augusta, Columbus and Savannah, Ga., Montgomery, Ala., and Columbia and Charleston, S.C.

During the '53 season, Aaron was expecting to join the Crackers the following year. Mann met him in Atlanta as Aaron was flying home to Mobile to report to the draft board. Mann was able to delay Aaron's draft physical, and the Hammer went to spring training with Milwaukee, played incredibly well and became the team's left fielder when Bobby Thomson broke his ankle.

A BLISTERING PRESEASON

In the meantime, Peeples was setting the '54 Crackers spring training camp and exhibition season on fire. In his first game, Peeples hit a pinch-hit double. He had a single and triple in two at-bats the next day and three days later hit a 400-foot homer. Then came three homers and almost a fourth over a two-game set. He arrived in Atlanta—for two weeks of exhibitions before the season opener—hitting .416.

All spring, Wyatt was cautioning Outlar and other

109

sportswriters to refrain from getting excited about Peeples. "He's not seen the curve ball yet," the old manager was quoted. Almost 7,000 people gave Peeples a warm welcome for his first exhibition game at Poncey, according to newspaper reports, as the Crackers hosted the Milwaukee Braves. Gene Conley was on the mound for the Braves, an old teammate of Peeples' at Elmira, and would have posted a no-hitter had it not been for Peeples, who got the Crackers' only hit of the game.

Peeples spared the Crackers the embarrassment of another no-hitter a week later by knocking a double off Wilmer "Vinegar Bend" Mizell, a major leaguer pitching for a Fort McPherson military team. Peeples' next time up, Mizell hung one right underneath his chin, and Peeples hit the ground before his bat.

While Peeples traveled with his team, he couldn't stay with in the same part of town as they did. "After every game there'd be someone from the team to pick me up and take me to the black section of town," Peeples said. "And the next day someone would come by and pick me up again, to take me to practice or the game.

"After the Milwaukee game, Mr. Mann himself took me to one of the black hotels," Peeples recalled. "He told me that he was trying to convince other teams in the league to bring a black player on board, but they told him that the time was not right for it.

"You couldn't find a better person than Earl Mann."

Jackie Robinson himself called Peeples twice, and "he kept telling me that I shouldn't lose my cool, that I should hang in there and everything would be all right. I wasn't angry about anything, but I was a little scared at times. If there were any death threats, I never knew about them. But I did know that I had to stick with it, because it had to be done, and I might as well have been the one to do it."

All of the Crackers accepted their new teammate, but the most support came from Chuck Tanner. "Nat Peeples was a good guy and

110

a good player," Tanner said. "But in those days, with the segregated stands and all that, the Southern Association just wasn't the place for a black man to play."

Peeples finished the exhibition schedule with a .333 average, six homers in 48 at-bats. Still, he wasn't on the starting roster when the '54 season opened in Mobile against the Bears. In the meantime, the Mobile owner had called Mann, complaining about some alleged game cancellations because of Peeples' presence. Mann, using his Southern Association ownership prerogative to look at the Bears' financial books, discovered only three cancellations with the team expecting one of its biggest opening nights ever.

Peeples did pinch hit in the fifth, and a Harwell Field crowd of 6,712, including 1,500 blacks sitting in the so-called colored bleachers, greeted him with a rousing round of applause, which drowned out the few scattered boos. He grounded weakly to the pitcher, while the Crackers went on to lose the game.

Bob Montag, who'd just been sent down to Atlanta by the Braves, had suffered a bruised hand during a Yankees' exhibition game (courtesy of Whitey Ford on the mound). Nonetheless, he went four-for-five during the opener, driving in seven runs.

"The next night, Mann tells Whit to start Peeples—in Alabama, of all places," Montag recalled. "Since left field is the only position Peeples practiced, Wyatt tells me, 'Tag, you'll have to sit out this game.' And I said, 'What? Are you crazy? I went four-for-five last night.'"

NEVER TO RETURN

Peeples went 0-for-four in the game. Two weeks later, he was optioned to the Class-A Jacksonville Red Caps, never to play a regular-season game at Ponce, return to Atlanta or even the Southern Association.

111

"Peeples was like the lamb going to the slaughterhouse," Montag said. "Nat was the best black player the Crackers had, and the management wanted a black ballplayer. He was just the wrong man at the right time."

"He was optioned to Jacksonville so he can play every day," said Mann, the day of Peeples' departure. "We feel that we have more experienced outfielders on the roster now who can be of more help to the club than Peeples. There definitely was no other reason for assigning him to Jacksonville. . . . I would not hesitate one second to bring another Negro into the league if he's good enough."

But despite Mann's assertions, rumors persisted that league pressure forced him to cut Peeples from the team. The fact is, keeping Nat Peeples on the team would have only intensified the racial tensions brewing like a cauldron in the segregated South. Birmingham, host to the Crackers' chief rival, also was home to Eugene "Bull" Connor, at the height of his racist demagoguery as the city's public safety commissioner. Blacks and whites, by municipal ordinance in Birmingham and state law in Louisiana, were prohibited from competing against each other. Vince Rizzo, general manager of the Pelicans during the 1950s, would have subjected himself to a jail sentence had he allowed Peeples to play his team when the Crackers traveled to New Orleans.

But life went on for Nat Peeples, who played 94 games in Jacksonville, finishing the season at .288. A ferocious swinger, he bounced around the Braves' farm system the next five years, rising as high as AAA.

During the off-seasons, he played winter ball in Columbia, Venezuela, Cuba and Panama. He played two-and-a-half seasons in the Class-AA Texas League before the Braves sold his contract in 1960 to the Mexico City Reds of the Mexican League, where his career ended in the middle of a .429 hitting streak.

"What hurt the most was that I was having a terrific season," Peeples said. "We were playing in Holigen, Texas, in a park that'd been converted from a football field to a baseball field. I was chasing down a fly ball and stepped into a hole. I fell, tore a bunch of ligaments in my knee. They had to carry me off the field on a stretcher, and the doctors told me they'd be able to repair the knee enough where I could walk, but probably never run again."

So ended the baseball career of Nathaniel Peeples, who walked a more turbulent, yet far less heralded, road than Robinson ever traveled. "Players make too much money today," he said. "I started out making $375 a month, and the most I ever made was $1,000 a month. But I was playing baseball, and I loved playing the game."

THE 518-MILE HOMER

The 1954 season was only a few days old when the first of many Southern Association records fell. On April 14 against the Chattanooga Lookouts, pitcher Leo Cristante set an all-time league record for participating in three double plays, the most ever for a pitcher. During that game, Atlanta set the all-time league record for most double plays in a game: six. The trio of Cristante, Billy Porter and Frank Torre fielded two, while Cristante, Torre and Paul Rambone had one. The rest were played by Rambone, Porter and Torre, Porter and Torre, and the sixth was fielded by Torre, unassisted.

Montag soon began earning his reputation as the Crackers' answer to Babe Ruth. He swung lefthanded, and before the year was over he would break the team record of 38 home runs set by Les Burge.

One particular homer made it out of the field—way out. A train was passing through on the tracks above the first-base line, and a Montag boomer landed in its coal car, 450 feet from home plate.

113

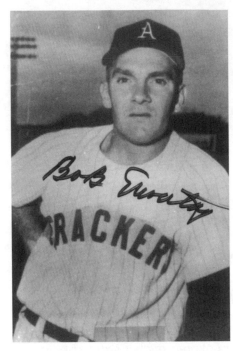

Bob Montag in 1954 when he set the record as the all-time Crackers home-run leader, with 39.

"A few days later our trainer told me there was some guy outside the locker room who wanted to see me," Montag said. "The train's fireman showed this ball that was covered with coal dust. He'd written on it, 'Atlanta to Nashville to Atlanta—518 Miles.' I autographed it for him."

One Saturday a month, the Crackers would hold baseball clinics for youngsters. "We had them from 10:30 until 1 P.M.," Montag said. "Kids would ask me, 'How do you hit a home run?' And I'd tell them, 'It's not easy, but you take a round ball and a round bat and hit it and then wait to see everyone's eyes pop out!'" And most of those kids wanted to be just like Bob Montag.

Tanner played every inning of every game that year, and lost 20 pounds over the season. Buck Riddle joined the team the same day he was released from the U.S. Army. He came down to Poncey, exchanged his Army greens for a Cracker uniform, and went five-for-five that night.

114

Even the pitchers got in on the hitting act. Dick Donovan set a team record for most home runs by a pitcher in a season: 12. "Three times I saw Donovan come into the game as a pinch hitter in the bottom of the ninth, and win the game with a hit," broadcaster Hank Morgan recalls. "I've never seen anything like it."

Donovan also had a reputation for being temperamental. Once, when Donovan was having a particularly rough outing, he noticed Wyatt leaving the dugout and heading to the mound to relieve him. Donovan fired the ball to Wyatt, who said, as the two men passed each other, "That was the hardest pitch you threw all night." Later, in the locker room, Wyatt backed the 6-foot-3-inch Donovan against the wall and said if he ever lost his temper like that again, his career would be over. The next season, Donovan signed with the White Sox and won 15 games.

On August 26, 1954, Cracker pitcher Glenn Thompson set the all-time Southern Association strikeout record when he fanned 19 New Orleans Pelicans. A 6-foot-5 giant with a furious sidearm delivery, he allowed only four hits and the Crackers won the game 4–2, giving up seven bases on balls. Every New Orleans player in the lineup struck out at least once, except pinch-hitter Bob Honor. But Pelican pitcher Bob Schultz also was tough to hit, striking out nine Crackers during the game.

At the All-Star game, the Crackers continued their dismantling of the league. They pounded manager Hugh Poland's visitors 9–1 before 16,808 people, the second-largest ever to see a Southern Association All-Star contest.

SMASHING THE RECORD BOOKS

When the season was over and done, Torre had set a league record for the most fielding chances by a first baseman

115

without an error, 1,006. Donovan went 17–11 and Don McMahon won 10 games and saved another 10. Cristante was the club's first 24-game winner in 25 years, and also was the league's top pitcher with a 3.59 ERA.

Montag, besides setting the team record in homers, finished the year with a .323 average, 109 RBIs and 122 base-on-balls. James Solt was the league's best-hitting catcher at .321. Second sacker Frank DiPrima led the league at his position with a .316 average, while Tanner finished .323 with 20 home runs and 101 RBIs.

The Crackers ended '54 at 94–60 (.610). The playoffs pit Atlanta against the fourth-place Memphis Chicks, and second-place New Orleans Pelicans against the Birmingham Barons, who finished third. Atlanta, after besting Memphis four games to two, met New Orleans, who'd defeated the Birmingham team by the same margin, in the finals. The Crackers beat the Pelicans four games to one, thus earning the right to play the Dixie Series against Houston, a team managed by their old skipper, Fred "Dixie" Walker.

116

The first two games were played in Atlanta, and the Crackers fared badly, losing both. "Those first games in Atlanta, they beat the hell out of us," Wyatt said. "I thought they'd brought a major league team in here."

Then came three games in Houston. "I called a meeting with our team," Wyatt remembered. "One particular player of theirs, a black fellow named Brown, was the one who was killing us. We were putting a young pitcher on the mound that day, and I told him and the team that a pitcher had to be a horse's ass. You had to be mean.

"The first time Brown came to bat, our pitcher knocked him back. He got up and dusted himself off, but that took the starch out of him." The Crackers won that game, lost the next, but won the fifth, thus trailing the series three games to two.

"We were at the Houston train depot after the fifth game, and I was sitting with Jasper Donaldson, the team secretary," Wyatt said. "Some of the boys came up to me and said, 'Skipper, we'll win two straight in Atlanta.' I thought they were being a little cocky."

Before the sixth game at Poncey, Furman Bisher of the *Atlanta Journal* made a visit to the Cracker locker room. "Bisher comes into the locker room about 10 or 15 minutes before the game started, and asked me who was going to pitch," Wyatt said. "I told him to wait a minute, and then I went over and asked Thompson if he could pitch on only a couple of days rest. He said, 'Skipper, I'm ready!' I pointed to him and yelled at Bisher, 'This is who's going to pitch today!'

"That's how a lot of those decisions were made back then."

WHITLOW'S GAME-GAMBLING HUNCH

Down 4–1 during the sixth game, the Crackers had the bases loaded and the mighty Montag was heading to the plate. "I knew Montag would hit their pitcher with a paddle," Wyatt said. "But something in my gut told me to put in Jim Solt, one of our relief pitchers. When I took Montag out, those fans booed me as bad as I've ever been booed. But when Solt hit that grand slam out of the park, that turned all of them around to my point of view."

"Whitlow told me he had a hunch and you couldn't go against that. What was important was we won the game," Montag said. And they won the next game as well, ending the incredible 1954 campaign.

Though Mann called the '41 team his "all-time favorite" because of its remarkable string of wins to start the season, the '54 team is arguably the greatest in franchise history.

"We had players on that '54 team that could play in today's big leagues," Tanner said. "Earl Mann paid me the major-league minimum in 1954 because he thought we could win it all.

117

After the season was over, he paid me an additional $1,000. My first year in the majors, I made less money than I did in my last year with the Crackers."

"In 1954, I had the best ballplayers ever put together on a field," said Wyatt, who passed away in 1999. "My managing had nothing to do with our season." But everyone who remembers or had anything to do with the season of '54 said that Whitlow Wyatt was the main reason the Atlanta Crackers accomplished a milestone that no other team in Southern Association baseball history ever did: win a 14th pennant, the Dixie Series and the Shaughnessy playoffs, thus hitting the Southern's grand slam for the second time.

THE MOST ELIGIBLE BACHELOR

Besides his professional team's second grand all-time slam, Earl Mann was treated to another joyous occasion in 1954, this one of a personal nature: making the acquaintance of an attractive Australian woman destined to become his third wife.

"I was in Atlanta visiting my cousin, and she told me she was going to introduce me to the most eligible bachelor in Atlanta," Myra Mann said. "Earl was very charismatic, a true Southern gentleman. He was powerful, but in a very quiet sort of way. He stood six-foot-three, tall and straight. He'd been going bald since he was 17, but he didn't care. He just combed his hair straight back.

"He was a great PR man, and loved the theater. He'd met many vaudeville stars, such as Mae West. He loved those people, and he'd go to New York to see them, and all of them knew him. He knew everyone on a first-name basis, from garbage men to governors. We saw each other again at the 1956 Melbourne Summer Olympics, and he went to every Olympic games after that. He loved athletics, though he wasn't athletic himself.

"He was a great baseball man, and could recognize talent when he saw it, unlike many owners today. He liked to sit in the stands with the people. I'd be sitting in these wonderful box seats, and he'd be walking the aisles, sitting and talking with the fans."

But all the public relations skills in the world couldn't brighten the dark days ahead for the Atlanta Crackers and the Southern Association.

119

GRAND SLAM!!

SEVENTH INNING

THE BEST BALLPLAYERS NEVER KNOWN

"You see, the ruling class always has its way. It's been like this throughout history, in America and in other parts of the world. We were considered inhuman, like objects with no heart or soul. That's why we were treated like we were. But when you're brought up like that, that's all you ever know."

—Norman F. Lumpkin, Atlanta Black Crackers

His teammates called him Geronimo because to them he was the fastest man alive. He was born in an Atlanta neighborhood nicknamed Buttermilk Bottom, some of which now is home to a parking lot for the Atlanta Civic Center. He had a good arm and was a natural right fielder, but back then one played where one was told, if not . . . well, let's put it like this: baseball was one of the very few avenues that led out of a cotton field for a black man.

Today, Norman F. Lumpkin lives in a clean, neatly kept house in northwest Atlanta, and his living room is full of books on the Negro American leagues. And if you ask him, he'll sit and regale you for days on end with tales of the greatest black baseball players who ever lived, some of whom played with him on the Atlanta Black Crackers from 1938–1948.

"Jackie Robinson was not the best black player around at the time," Lumpkin said. "But Branch Rickey chose the right man to break the color barrier because of Robinson's temperament. There were black players back then who would have killed someone if they'd put up with half the abuse Robinson had to put up with.

"And I'll tell you, enduring all of that mistreatment probably shortened Robinson's life."

THE BEGINNINGS OF BLACK BASEBALL

Baseball didn't begin segregated. In the 19th century, black ballplayers appeared on integrated teams and some black teams played in integrated leagues. In 1867, the same year in which Atlanta University was chartered and Summer Hill School (now Clark-Atlanta University) opened, the Uniques of Brooklyn hosted the Philadelphia Excelsiors in a contest billed as the "championship of colored clubs." The Excelsiors triumphed in this post-Civil War battle, 37–24.

In 1868, the Pythian Base Ball Club then applied for entry into the National Association of Base Ball Players, the first organized professional major league. Their application would be futile, as the nominating committee unanimously rejected their application, as they would an application by "any club composed of one or more colored persons," the committee said. And, "if colored clubs were admitted there would be, in all probability, some division of feeling, whereas by excluding them no injury could result to anyone," it added. This was the first appearance of an official color line in baseball.

The sport of baseball was first popularized in Atlanta's black community by college athletes, such as these circa-1900 Morris Brown College players.
Library of Congress

In 1871, the National Association of Base Ball Clubs officially banned blacks from playing in its all-white league. The first organized all-black semi-pro team was born in 1885, when the Cuban Giants were formed by waiters of the Argyle Hotel in Babylon, N.Y., to entertain hotel guests.

In the 1880s, the League of Colored Baseball Players was formed. At about the same time, black baseball in Atlanta was born in the early 1880s at Atlanta University, Clark University and other colleges in the city. It was the first sport ever organized at Atlanta Baptist College (now Morehouse College) in 1890. That

123

team was put together by D.D. Crawford, and included Alfred D. Jones, Peter James Bryant, W.E. Rainwater and E.P. Epps.

From 1890 to 1897, Atlanta University went undefeated save for one loss at the hands of the dreaded Baptists in 1893. In 1895, baseball was the only sport allowed on the campus of Morris Brown College. The first team was organized by Willis Lane, a student who also served as coach. Other players to wear the school's purple and black were E.K. Nichols and Charles L. Harper.

In 1896, Atlanta Baptist's James A. Nabrit organized the Atlanta Baseball League consisting of all the Negro colleges. A silk pennant was given to the winner at the end of the season. Each school played six games. Clark was permitted to include students from Gammon Theological Seminary, while Morris Brown could use outsiders. The Atlanta Baptist Tigers won the league championship in 1896, 1897 and 1898. In 1900, Alfred D. Jones became the first baseball coach ever hired by the school, and would lead the team to its fourth baseball championship in five years.

While Atlanta's black college students were playing baseball, Atlanta's first black professional team, the Deppens, was touring the South before the turn of the century. They played teams from New Orleans, Birmingham, Macon and Chattanooga. The Deppens eventually were succeeded by the Atlanta Cubs, a semipro team composed of black college students from various local schools.

THE RED SUMMER AND THE BLACK CRACKERS

The middle of 1919, later called "the Red Summer," was a time of racial tension throughout the country, as 26 violent race riots broke out in several Southern towns, as well as in Chicago, New York City, and Washington, D.C. The Atlanta Black Crackers were born in this atmosphere.

The team was actually the former Atlanta Cubs, who decided to re-christen themselves the Black Crackers simply because that's what many fans called them. The team's owner was William J. Shaw, a local restaurateur who operated an establishment called the Roof Garden.

In March 1920, the Black Crackers joined the Negro Southern League, which was made up of New Orleans Crescent Stars, Montgomery Grey Sox, Jacksonville Red Caps, Nashville Elite Giants, Birmingham Black Barons and the Memphis Red Sox. The Black Crackers stayed in the league and represented the city through 1936.

The Atlanta Black Crackers and their league were generally con-sidered to be farm teams to the black baseball leagues that operated nationally. In 1920, the National Association of Colored Baseball Clubs was founded by Andrew "Rube" Foster; the organization would later become the Negro National League. Foster himself had been a massively built pitcher who once led his Chicago-American Giants to a 123–6 record. He once quoted his pitching philosophy when runners were on base: "Do not worry. Try to appear jolly and uncon-cerned. I have smiled often with the bases full with two strikes and three balls on the batter. This seems to unnerve. In other instances, where the batter appears anxious to hit, waste a little time on him and when you think he realizes his position and everybody is yelling at him to hit it out, waste a few balls and try his nerve; the majority of times you will win him out by drawing him into hitting a wide one."

Foster organized his league because of baseball's custom of banning black ballplayers from big league professional teams. After a rocky start, the Negro Leagues grew into one of the largest, best-known black-owned businesses in America.

The Atlanta Black Crackers played their games at Morehouse College, Morris Brown College, and Ponce de Leon Ball Park, when the white Crackers weren't there. One of its early

125

stars was Christobel Torrienti, a muscular Cuban who stood 5 feet 10 inches and weighed close to 200 pounds. A left-hand hitter, he could hit powerfully toward all directions but was especially strong in pulling the ball to right field.

Another member of the early Black Crackers was Arthur Idlett. "We got the best players from Morehouse, Morris Brown and Clark, and organized the Black Crackers," Idlett recalled in an interview with Bernard West for the book *Living Atlanta: An Oral History of the City*. "Then school closed [for the summer] and we started barnstorming."

Barnstorming was a way for black baseball teams to supplement their income, and they often traveled thousands of miles each year by car, bus or trains. "Most of the time we were on trains," Idlett recalled. "We went down to New Orleans; Hattiesburg and Meridian, Mississippi; Birmingham and Montgomery, Alabama; and Columbus, Augusta and Gainesville, Georgia."

 126 BARNSTORMING ALL OVER THE NATION

Small towns on the barnstorming circuit gave the visiting teams the most enthusiastic welcomes. And the crowds weren't all black. "Plenty of white people [came] in these small towns," Idlett said. "You see, you start closing the store down on half a day on Wednesdays. And that was the big day in small towns, baseball day, [and] we'd have big crowds. That's the only activity they had. They didn't have any clubs and shows and all that stuff going on. They had going to church and baseball games, and they went to baseball games."

And the players were particularly popular with the local female populations. "These girls were crazy about baseball," Idlett said. "They're crazy about athletes and stuff like that, but especially baseball players. They would have dances after the baseball game and of course that would help the manager raise money. And you meet all them girls around the baseball game.

"Small towns produced some beautiful women. You had either a Masonic hall, Elks hall . . . and you had to be able to have a dance at all those places. And sometimes the musicians would be barnstorming, too, and they would ride along with the baseball team. And a lot of times the band would be at the baseball game playing while the game was going on, to drum up crowds for the dance that night, and help the baseball team." Later, bands would divide up the receipts with the athletes.

In Chattanooga, against the Choo Choos, Idlett was on the same field as Satchel Paige. "Now, we didn't know anything about Satchel Paige then," he said. "[But] Paige would throw that ball so hard, his catcher couldn't hold him, and we were running on that third strike, and that's the way we beat the Chattanooga Choo Choos, because we had more pure speed than they did.

"We were just having a good time then, not making money, but just playing baseball. It was fun playing baseball then."

Paige was a friend of James "Gabby" Kemp, who joined the Atlanta Black Crackers in 1935, and who spent 10 to 15 years barnstorming across the nation. In an interview with West, Kemp remembered a May 1935 trip to the south Georgia town of Thomaston: "They had a beautiful parade, and a big old beautiful park and barbecues, they would start running barbecues and parades, and oh, down in those small towns, they had good race relations down there and those folks just go in there and say, 'Hey, John,' 'Hey, there,' 'Hey, ballplayer.' Oh, the food, they would have tables spread out like a family reunion or something like that for our ball club, very clean, good food, lemonade and all that stuff.

"And we had to play a doubleheader. Well, each ballplayer was a man, so I took him as a man, a feeling man, and he would know how much he wanted to eat during intermissions. So I said, 'If your stomach starts hurting, you lose your job. If

127

your stomach causes you to lose your job, just go eat like a hog.' But they didn't do that. They know how much, out in that hot sun, how much to eat."

THE HARDSHIPS OF LIFE ON THE ROAD

While barnstorming paid the players good money, it was a life full of hardships. Buses were forever breaking down. "The buses [we] used weren't the type of buses we have now, that can go 300 to 400 miles without having mechanical trouble," said Kemp. "Sometimes the bus would break down on the highway and there you were. You had to sleep in the bus without water to take a bath or to wash up, and you had to eat out of chairs.

"And then when we did get to the restaurant . . . we had to line up at the back window and wait to get whatever they would sell us, back in the back. Then we'd park our bus around on the side of the front of the place to eat whatever we brought there or whatever we had to eat. If you had a roommate, you would buy some type of food and he would buy the other type of food and then we would divide the food together and have a meal. Then we'd get back in the bus and ask the man who managed the place if we could go sleep while the mechanic repaired the damages."

Then there were the problems with sleeping accommodations. "In those days the hotels owned and operated by Negroes were few, and you had to get to a town [and] maybe ask the manager of the hotel for maybe two or three rooms," Kemp recalled. "And the ballplayers would go in, as many as they could, and just lie across the bed and go to sleep. Sometimes in the big, larger cities, we stopped at the YMCA."

Negro Southern League franchises were not even close to being financially stable. The visiting and home teams each furnished two balls per game, and games often had to be stopped to retrieve the balls.

"Baseballs cost about $15 a dozen, and that was a lot of money then," Idlett said. "So we tried to protect our balls. We'd get a little talcum powder when we stopped playing and try to clean the ball up . . . for the next game." Uniforms came from colleges and the white Atlanta Crackers, who gave their black counterparts their old ones.

"Yet those teams that were playing Negro baseball had some good equipment," Kemp said. "They weren't ragged and their uniforms were very neatly kept, cleanly and they wore a uniform very proudly. When we came on the field . . . we did look respectable and the people appreciated what the baseball players during those days were trying to do to improve baseball."

The home team reimbursed the visiting team's travel expenses from gate receipts. Since the teams only carried about 12 players, the athletes played more than one position, and membership on teams changed constantly. Relief pitchers were non-existent, and after working a few innings on the mound, pitchers moved to the outfield to finish out the game.

"Most teams carried about three pitchers," Idlett said. "That pitcher could pitch every third day, and we didn't know nothing about tired and all that kind of stuff. They would get sore arms and each one would rub the other down with mustard roll. And we made a concoction out of alcohol and black pepper. But they pitched every third or fourth day."

"We would play seven to 10 ballgames a week," Kemp said, "and our ballplayers had to be strong and stable. You have to be in good physical condition riding from town to town. Sometimes we'd ride all night to get to the town the next day, and then we would play. . . . If we hit a town 120 miles from the night game, we would play in that town Saturday afternoon and without changing. The only thing we would change would be our socks and sweatshirts. We

129

would keep our luggage in our bus and the two teams would ride . . . to the next town and play that night, which would make two games in one day."

"ALL THEM DUCKS GOT THE MONEY"

As bad as the teams' money woes were, it was even worse for the players. "We used to say, de ducks got all the money," Idlett said. "Deductions, you see. When we play a team, they take out for the base-balls, they take out for the umpires, they take out for the park. . . . Deductions, and we nicknamed it 'de ducks.' All them ducks got the money. So if there were anything left over, then you would divide it equally among the players. Sometimes they got 50 cents, 75 cents or a dollar, or something like that."

Often the black players couldn't play on the same diamonds used by whites, even if whites weren't using the field at the time. "So we had to get some place that the man had roped off and play," Kemp said. "In those days we called them cow pastures. But we made out and we would get the money. They would have some type of stands built there and they would sell cold drinks and fish sandwiches and fried pies and things like that, and then they would have a rope. And you could get in the ballpark, but they would pass the hat. And they would have admission, have a little box here, a gate there, where you come through there, but people would just walk on across the pastures and just get on behind the rope, and sometimes they would just put in a quarter or whatever they had."

Players also had to dress in the homes they lived in, because they weren't allowed to use the white dressing rooms. Bill Yancey, star shortstop for the Black Yankees, Philadelphia Stars, Hillsdale, and the Lincoln Giants, recalled a barnstorming trip to Rome in 1945: "I'm the manager and I got to find out where you dress. So I asked this guy, who looked like a half-wit who was taking care of the clubhouse,

130

'Where can my boys dress?' He said, 'Well, you niggers have to go down to some of those houses down the road and get dressed.'"

Many people in the small towns in which the team barnstormed would take them in for the few days the Black Crackers would be playing. "They would take the ballplayers in for rent and . . . they would have good, old-fashioned home-type cooked food that we call soul food, man, it was a blast," Kemp said. "The eating was beautiful and the folk were beautiful."

CANNIBALS AND BIBLICAL HEROES

In 1923, Ed Bolden formed the Eastern Colored League, and together with Foster's organization, they would operate successfully for several years. In 1924, Booker T. Washington High, Atlanta's first black public school, opened. Two years later, the black newspaper *Atlanta Daily World,* published its first edition. The zenith of the Negro National Leagues came at the same time, as major-league black players commanded salaries of more than $350 a month, almost incomprehensible wages by the standards of most African-American wage earners at the time.

The Atlanta Black Crackers also played against the great Negro independent league teams. The House of David came through. And the Zulu Cannibal Giants. "The Zulus were a team [that wore] a uniform made like the skirts of the Zulu tribes," Idlett recalled. "All that was just for a drawing card."

The Zulus were from Florida, many of them from Miami. "The skirts were imported from Hawaii, and underneath them they had short pants with sliding pads and the other protectors next to their skin," said Gabby Kemp. "And they had wigs. They wore wigs and were made up like cannibals or had paint all over their faces, yet they had some of the best baseball players on this team, the Zulu Cannibal Giants, in America."

131

◇

Kemp also saw the Benton Harbor, Mich.-based House of David. The religious movement by the same name sought to spread its word with its barnstorming team. "It was composed of Negroes and Cubans . . . and they had some Negro ballplayers who were outstanding. They grew whiskers and looked like . . . those biblical photographs."

When the Great Depression came, however, it destroyed whatever prosperity black baseball players were enjoying. And the Negro Southern League suffered as well. But while colleges ceased their baseball programs, sandlot games kept going.

Still, in 1933 a new Negro National League was formed, and the Negro American League was chartered in 1937. These two leagues thrived until the color line was broken. During their existence, the Negro Leagues played eleven World Series (1924–27, 1942–48) and created their own All-Star game (1933–48) that became the biggest black sports attraction in the country.

 Also in the mid '30s, Webster Baker, a teacher at Atlanta's Booker T. Washington High School, and his business partner, Percy Williams, formed an Atlanta Black Cracker squad with players such as Donald Reeves and Kemp who, in particular, had enjoyed an outstanding academic and sports career at Morris Brown. Kemp posted varsity letters in baseball, track, basketball, football and debate, and was the only student in school history to receive five letters in one year.

"I was a member of a team here in Atlanta called the Tigers," Kemp recalled, "a group of young boys and youths from the ages of 12–18. And we won some championships, and I was elected by a man, namely [team business manager] W.B. Baker, to become a member of the Atlanta Black Crackers."

As a member of the Negro Southern League, the Atlanta Black Crackers finally gained major league status in 1932, but only played eight games, winning one and losing seven. Kemp joined the Atlanta

Black Crackers in 1935 as a shortstop at age 19, and would spend all but one season with Atlanta between 1935–1947, and later toured with Jackie Robinson's all-stars in 1949. The team was owned by Michael Shane when Kemp joined the squad; shortstop Ormand Sampson was his manager.

The 1935 Black Crackers also saw the arrival of pitcher/outfielder/first baseman/third baseman Felix "Chin" Evans, who spent the prior season playing for the semi-pro Atlanta Athletics. The hard-throwing right-hander spent 16 years in black baseball, including stints with the Jacksonville Red Caps (1938); Indianapolis ABCs (1939); Newark Eagles (1939); Ethiopian Clowns (1939–40); Memphis Red Sox (1940–48); and Birmingham Black Barons (1949). But his career began in his hometown of Atlanta with a overhand curve pitch which he called his "mountain drop."

Also joining the Black Crackers in '35 was first baseman James "Red" Moore. "We didn't play nighttime baseball back then, so we'd be out in the sun all day long," Moore recalled. "My light-colored skin would turn red, and that's how I got my nickname." Moore played ball at Booker T. Washington High, and in 1934 began a semipro career with the Macon Peaches before signing with Atlanta the next year.

The '35 Black Crackers opened the season with George Clifford "Jew Baby" Bennette as manager. Bennette was in the twilight of his career, which began in 1920 with Columbus Buckeyes, then followed with stints with the Detroit Stars, Pittsburgh Keystones, Indianapolis ABCs, and the Chicago-American Giants in 1936. As manager of the '35 Black Crackers, he was fired after only 10 games.

A MAN WHO KNEW PSYCHOLOGY

James Greene, a Stone Mountain native, joined the team in 1936 and stayed until '39 (after a stint with the Kansas City Monarchs, he returned to Atlanta and took a job at the

133

Sears & Roebuck store across the street from Poncey). A year later, the Atlanta Black Crackers had a new owner.

In 1937, Reverend John H. Harden and his wife, Billie, owners of Harden's Service Station on Auburn Avenue, purchased an interest in the team from Michael Shane. "[They] had a beautiful filling station in front of their home," Kemp recalled. "Mr. and Mrs. Harden were two very nice people and their friendship with the ball club was astounding. Our ball club was more like a family, a close-knit family, one for all and all for one, something like the old musketeer slogan."

"W.B. Baker owned the team at that time, and he was having a little difficulty in getting the players around, because he didn't have a bus," recalled Billie Harden, in an interview with West. "Mr. Baker was a friend of ours. We had met him in our filling station business. And he would come in from time to time, maybe getting gas or what have you with the team. Then they began getting friendly and he would talk to my husband about it, that he needed a little help along the line, and of course he could hardly manager with the team because . . . he had no finances. And we had very little, but we decided . . . to give it a try. And of course Mr. Baker, with his knowledge about the club, he did help [us] all he could about the operation of it.

"[Baker] just sort of got disgusted with it, and when he did, my husband decided to buy the team. And of course this meant that we had to really sort of start at the bottom and try to work our way through all of it."

The Hardens became the team's sole owners in 1938. "John Harden was a hellraiser before he became a reverend," Lumpkin remembered. "But he knew psychology, and he knew how to get things done." Baker continued to serve as the team's business manager.

The couple had been around baseball all their lives, Harden himself having played the game in school. "But I don't know if either of us had any particular interest at that time," Mrs. Harden said. "All the ballplayers would gather around the filling station . . . discussing baseball, and I think it sort of built a little interest in my husband."

"Mr. Harden bought the best equipment because Mrs. Harden . . . wanted the best because they had always been accustomed to the best," Kemp said. "So we got the best equipment, the best-looking uniforms that money could buy, and our practice uniforms, our spring training uniforms, [were] ordered according to the ballplayers we had. So Mr. Harden would buy the best equipment, the best protectors. We bought the same things that the major league ballplayers [bought]."

And the Hardens made sure their players never missed a payday. "If we were on the road, if Mrs. Harden wasn't there, she would wire me expense money," Kemp remembered. "Each ballplayer was allotted so much money per day to eat. They had the money in their pockets.

"Mr. Harden was a man that if he said something, his word was his bond and he usually performed and did what he said he was going to do. He was a great man and a pure man."

"I HAVE NEVER MET A FINER MAN IN ALL MY LIFE"

Along with a more secure income, the Hardens also negotiated with Earl Mann for the use of Ponce de Leon Ball Park when the white Crackers were away. "He really did make it easy for me, because he was congenial," vice president and treasurer Billie Harden said. "If we had any problem I could take it to Mr. Mann, and he really made it easy for me as a owner here. He was always very considerate, and whenever I'd go to his office he gave me due respect. I mean, he would ask me to sit down, and this was not the thing all of them were doing at that time. And we'd sit down and talk, anything pertaining to the park or to the clubs or what have you.

"He was just always a very considerate man. He had a big

135

The Atlanta Black Crackers' Norman Lumpkin was considered one of the fastest players in the game. He played all outfield positions and was lead-off batter his entire career from 1938–49.

heart in him. He wanted to help all he could. That was more than I could say about some of the others I heard speaking in the same situation. I have never met a finer man in all my life."

"At my ball games, we drew plenty of white people, all walks and professions of life, and they just come in and sit down," Kemp said. "Just come in and sit down. Nobody paid any attention, and to watch my ballclub play, 'cause they knew they were going to see some real ball. At that time the Atlanta Crackers were declining and to keep baseball alive we had to put on a show out there for those people to keep them interested in seeing our team play.

"There weren't any racial tensions, wasn't any fights or anything. We never had a fight out there."

Still, the park's facilities remained off limits to the black team. "We weren't allowed to use the dressing facilities or the showers, so we'd dress at home before the game and take a shower at home after the game," Lumpkin said. And the stadium remained segregated during the white Crackers' games, with blacks having to reach their left-field bleacher seats through a side entrance underneath the white section.

136

SEVENTH-INNING STRETCH

TAKE ME OUT TO THE BALLGAME...

LEROY "Satchell" PAIGE

Leroy "Satchel" Paige appeared on this
1949 Bowman bubble gum card.

GABBY KEMP REMEMBERS SATCH

"He would come to Atlanta and down on Auburn Avenue they had a grill called Big Smitty's Grill and everybody, white and colored, wanted to see the mighty Satchel Paige.

"Satchel Paige could throw so hard and so mysteriously that sometimes the ball would get there before you knew the ball was there. . . . If you were afraid of fastballs, you were afraid of Satchel Paige. But he never hit anybody, never did, because one lick in your ribs with the type of ball he threw . . . would paralyze you for life and probably kill you.

"When he came to Atlanta our purses went up, because he was a drawing card on Auburn, he was a drawing card on the baseball diamond, he was a friend to all the children, the youth, the students out there at that ballpark, and when we played the Kansas City Monarchs, we made money. If we played them in Macon, we made money. If we played them in Waycross, we made money. Satchel Paige coming to town—people started coming to the ballpark at 4:30 and 5:00.

"One of my greatest thrills I've had in my life in baseball was I hit a home run 340 feet in the left-field bleachers off Leroy "Satchel" Paige, right out there at Ponce de Leon Ball Park. And Satchel Paige pointed his finger at me, saying 'I will never trust a turkey any more.' So in that game I came up again. I was the fourth man up, two men out. He walked the bases loaded, and he called his outfielders about six yards from the infield.

"The first pitch he threw me was a sidearm fastball about as fast as a rifle bullet on the outside corner. [Umpire] B.T. Harvey said, 'Strike *one!*' I got out of the box, I said, 'Umpire, you need some glasses.' . . . So he threw me a ball outside, ball outside, three balls and one strike. My classmates at Morris Brown, those I knew at Morehouse and all the people on Auburn and throughout Atlanta were saying, 'Come on, come on, baby, slap one!'

"And I'm up there, and Satchel's looking at me like a tiger stalking a little lamb. Satchel had an unorthodox type of delivery that came sidearm, which we call crossfire, stepping toward third base. And he stepped toward third base and fired that ball, and the ball was hitting the outside corner. That was strike two. And he told the outfield to sit down.

"So I'm up there, waving my bat, digging in. I'm looking for the ball, and the ball was on its way up there and he walking on toward the dugout, and Mr. Harvey said, 'Strike *three!*' And the crowd broke down in havoc. Boy, they applauded Satchel Paige and gave him a standing ovation. And they gave me the boos. Just two innings before, I was a hero. Now he struck me out. Who hadn't he struck out? He'd struck out everybody in the world!"

1 2 3 4 5 6 7 **8** 9 10

GOING, GOING, GONE!

E I G H T H   I N N I N G

BLACK CRACKERS AND ABCs

"The Black Cracker ball club [that] was one of the best ball clubs baseball has ever seen in the North or South was the Black Cracker club of 1938. This team was well rounded. This was one of the best baseball teams with the best baseball talent, man for man, that I believe has been put together in Atlanta, Georgia, up until the present day."

—James "Gabby" Kemp

In 1938 the Atlanta Black Crackers merged their Negro Southern League franchise into the Negro American League, and were destined to make a run at history. At the beginning of the spring there were two separate teams vying to represent the city in the Negro American League. Eventually, though, the two squads merged into a single team called the Atlanta Black Crackers, a team that would include many heralded athletes.

Pitcher Chin Evans was a freshman at Morehouse College when the '38 season began, but had to remain home when the team traveled so

◇

he wouldn't miss classes. Management subsequently dropped him from the roster, so he signed with the Jacksonville Red Caps and became a big winner, including notching a victory over his old team. Within a month the Black Crackers had negotiated for his return.

Also on the spring roster was rookie right-handed pitcher Eddie "Bullet" Dixon, a hard-throwing fastballer with explosive speed and good control. He also utilized a fast curve and a slider. In the spring he shut out the U.S. Army team, 15–0. Shortstops Sampson and Dick Lundy were also on hand. Other players on the spring roster but who were released for one reason or another by May included pitchers Roosevelt Brown and James Brown, both from Tennessee; pitcher James "Black Rider" Brown; Mute Barnes, a big left-hander; William Black, an outfielder from Jackson, Miss.; and Roy Burke, another pitcher.

"The Atlanta baseball caravan for 1938 set forth yesterday afternoon at Washington Park where [Vinicus] 'Nish' Williams and 18 hopefuls started the long grind that will last until autumn is almost back upon us," wrote the *Atlanta Daily World* on April 5. But bad weather hampered the team's conditioning regime, and soon the team left Atlanta for a 10-day training venture staying in a training camp at Fort Benning, Ga.

"Camp Benning offers a splendid site for a baseball outfit with miles and miles separating the boys from the sidewalks of city life and consequent mischief," wrote the *Atlanta Daily World*'s sports editor Ric Roberts. "The collegians now in school will not be able to stay away from lecture hours a week so Manager Williams will be shy Kemp, [William] Cooper, Pope, Hadley and Foster during most of the trip which shifts to Augusta the latter part of the week."

The '38 Black Crackers opened their exhibition season by defeating the Alabama Wild Cats in Columbus, Ga., 7–1. Kemp had three hits and scored four runs. Four different pitchers took the mound that day. The next day, the Black Crackers won again 7–1 against a hometown Columbus team.

Williams quickly found himself in a quandary, however. He had two excellent first basemen: Jim Canady and Red Moore. "What made Manager Nish [Williams] utter right out loud was the way Canady and Moore, bitter rivals for the first base position, kicked that sack in the Sunday game," reported the *Atlanta Daily World*. "Canady was an expert and left nothing to be desired in his sparkling display. Moore was the same fancy first baseman who was the talk of the National League and New York last summer. This is bound to be the toughest decision that Nish must make. Many ball clubs would like to have either man and when one is finally disposed it will be for a fancy price. Canady may be kept for utility duty or even third base play if Sampson changes his mind in favor of the Chicago-American Giants." Moore's fielding and hitting eventually won him the spot.

Black Semi-Pro Teams in Atlanta
Atlanta All-Stars
Atlanta Deppens
Atlanta Tigers
Ashby Street All-Stars
Reed Street Tigers
Aiken Omega
Herndon Blue Devils
Highs Harlem Inn
Ivey Brothers
Hanley Hornets
Globe Trotters
Haugabrooks
University Eagles

A few days later they took on a team from Fort Benning, where many black soldiers were assigned. The contest wasn't even close— 23–3, in favor of the Black Crackers, with Bullet Dixon striking out 12 in six innings. The next two days kept the Black Crackers undefeated, beating Columbus 10–0 and 10–4.

Then came a chance for the team to see how it measured up to the best team in all of black organized baseball. "The lid flies up this afternoon at Ponce de Leon Park promptly at 3 o'clock where the Atlanta Black Crackers will march to battle face to face with the greatest colored baseball team in the world (and that means a better club than at least ten major league white clubs you could name), those Homestead Grays," stated the April 24 edition of the *Atlanta Daily World.* The previous year, the Grays were the Negro National League champions, and in fact won seven titles over the course of a decade. The team had many stars, notably Josh Gibson. The Black Crackers were swept, by scores of 4–1, 6–3, and 8–4.

Next on the schedule was a nine-game, 10-day barnstorming trip, which included dropping four straight games to the Memphis Red Sox. The Chicago-American Giants then came to town, sweeping the Black Crackers in two games. Doubts clouded the Black Crackers' horizon as the regular season began.

A MOTHER TO THE TEAM

Billie Harden also began traveling with the team while on the road. "She would travel with the ball club to those towns in which the gate was going to be 10 or 12 or 15 or 20 thousand people, and she learned the [system] they used," Kemp said. "She'd be there so the ducks wouldn't get us and she would be there when they checked that money up. They stopped ducking on the Black Crackers, 'cause Mrs. Harden got hip to the jive they was putting down with the ducks.

"She traveled with the ball club just like one of us, and was good in company 'cause we would tease and talk just like that, and a fellow got used to good English other than *damn* or something like that."

If any player got out of line with un-gentlemanly behavior, his teammates had a way of disciplining him. "We had a few that were not so nice," Billie Harden recalled, "but [the team] had a way of sort of getting on them, in a nice little way. They would just put him aside. They would just sort of abandon them and let them be a loner for a long time. We just wouldn't have anything to do with them until they could get their attitude right. That's the way we disciplined ballplayers back then."

"Sometimes they would make a mistake and say things out of line. And I was quite understanding, because me being a woman with a bunch of men, I realized sometimes they would forget a lady was around. And I would always forgive them. But it would have to be something pretty rough that the ballplayers resented it themselves. But they all respected me and I respected them. I was sort of like a mother for them."

By the time the season was halfway through, the Atlanta Black Crackers were in fourth place, behind Memphis, the Kansas City Monarchs, and the Indianapolis ABCs. Teams didn't play the same number of league-credited games, and the Black Crackers record in that category was 9–10.

The team's management was so embarrassed by the players' performance that it took out an apologetic ad in local newspapers. The ad read

> *The Atlanta Black Cracker baseball club wishes to convey this message of thanks to the several thousands of fans who have supported the 1938 season despite its many unfortunate interludes. The going has been tough all the way with injuries to key men plus the loss of stars like Ping Burke, Sampson, Kemp, Red Moore and Dick Lundy for many days . . . all of these factors contributed to a difficult situation. The first half is ended. The second half begins in Atlanta next Sunday against Indianapolis. The club plans to continue rebuilding until a winning outfit is realized. While this period of forced experimentation is transpiring, we have nothing but thanks for your kind indulgence.*

The Hardens were also skilled in the art of public relations. "[Billie Harden] would send us to radio shows and have interviews, and talk," Kemp said. "And then we would help different youth organizations, both white and colored."

145

THE SECOND-HALF RUN

By the time the second half of the '38 season arrived, second baseman Kemp had been promoted to manager, and the Atlanta Black Crackers would go on to win the second-half title, a run which featured 19 straight wins.

Several players who signed on for the season's second half were instrumental in the team's championship run. Thomas "Pee Wee" Butts was a star quarterback for Booker T. Washington High when the Black Crackers signed him out of school in 1938. As the new short-stop, he provided a spark for the team, showing the skills that would make him into an outstanding defensive infielder—a steady glove, sure hands, exceptional range and a strong, accurate throwing arm that was specially made for the double play.

Right-handed pitcher James "Ping" Burke rejoined the Black Crackers for the second half of '38. Originally from Greensboro, Ga., Burke was a fastball artist with excellent speed and a fast curve-ball. He had joined the Black Crackers two years earlier, and his 1937 season was outstanding, which included a 13-strikeout, three-hit shutout of the Chicago-American Giants. A contract dispute at the start of the next season sent Burke to the semipro Athens (Ga.) Red Sox. But when he finally did sign for the Black Crackers in time for the second half of '38, he would often tire in the late innings.

Another player who returned to the Black Crackers of '38 was Red Moore who, since his first Black Cracker season in '35, had played for the Mohawk Giants of Schenectady, N.Y., before signing with the Newark Eagles for the remainder of the '36 season. The next year he was a member of the "million-dollar infield" for the Eagles, which con-sisted of second baseman Dick Seay; shortstop Willie Wells (who Lumpkin described as "the measuring stick for a lot of black ballplayers back then"); third baseman Ray Dandridge; and catcher Leon Ruffin. This combination gave the Eagles a gold-glove man at

The Atlanta Black Crackers of 1938.
Negro Leagues Baseball Museum

each position. Moore also held his own at the plate, recording a .280 average for the '37 season.

Kemp paired with shortstop Pee Wee Butts to form a solid middle-infield combination. Along with first baseman Rob Moore, the team had a tight infield. Sluggers Babe Davis, Don Pelham and Joe "Pig" Greene furnished the run production for 1938. Pitchers Bo Mitchell, Chin Evans and Twelosh Howard handled most of the mound chores for the club. Also on the club that year were William Cooper and Red Handley. Pitcher James Brooks was signed for the second half of '38 but didn't receive much playing time.

"Red Moore was our first baseman when I joined the team," Butts said. "He was one of the greatest fielders I saw in a long time. Pig Greene had a good arm, could throw, could get the ball to you on time so the runner wouldn't have a chance to go through his act and spike you or something like that."

147

Chin Evans was a big winner for the Black Crackers in the playoffs. Late in the baseball season, when college football practice was beginning, Evans would often double up on his sports and, on one occasion, left football practice to pitch a postseason victory over the Birmingham Black Barons.

The second half of the season began with a series against the ABCs, the first game of which was a rain-out. In a Sunday doubleheader, the Black Crackers won by scores of 9–3 and 5–4. Then came a road trip to Birmingham, Louisville, and Indianapolis. They beat the Birmingham Black Barons 8–5 but lost the next day. The *Atlanta Daily World* showed the Black Crackers in first place in the Negro American League.

Then it was on to Louisville, a non-league contest against the Colonels. Atlanta lost, 6–2. The Indianapolis games were canceled because of rain, so the team moved on, playing a series of semi-pro teams in Illinois. On the way home, they split two games with Indianapolis, and remained in first place.

In late July, the Black Crackers defeated the Fort Benning team 11–2, in front of about 1,000 spectators. The next game they faced an all-star team of semi-pros from all over the nation, including Big Jimmy Reese and Roughhouse Haynes, a former Morehouse All-American football player. The game, played at Booker T. Washington High School Stadium, went to the Black Crackers, 5–3.

Fans of the Black Crackers gave Red Moore a special day at the ballpark in his honor, on the last day of July, before a doubleheader with the Nashville Elite Giants. "The Prince of First Basemen" was given a $25 mitt, a pair of $6 white Oxfords, a $40 radio, a case of Wheaties, a case of beer, two baseball bats (from Earl Mann), a fried chicken, a baked ham, a deluxe cake, several neckties, and some small cash donations. "I also remember getting a couple of suits," Moore said. "I was one well-dressed cat."

Mann also told Moore "that I ought to go to Cuba and learn how to speak a little Spanish, you know, and probably I could change my nationality, you understand, from black to some other. I said, 'No, it wouldn't do for me to do nothing like that—people in Atlanta know me.'"

The Black Crackers swept the Nashville doubleheader, even though Moore didn't have a good day at the plate, going hitless in seven at-bats, yet still scoring a run in the second game. By the end of July he was hitting .331, and at season's end, he was selected to the Southern News Service's Negro American League All-Star Game.

Next up were the Jacksonville Red Caps, in Florida; the Chicago-American Giants; and a barnstorming tour throughout the midwest, often against white semi-pro teams in Indiana, Wisconsin and Illinois. In Muncie, Ind., they split a doubleheader against the state champs, a team called the Corn Top Giants. Next was Elkhart, Ind., and finally the Chicago-American Giants, resulting in an 8–7 loss. Two days later, the Black Crackers went back to Milwaukee to defeat the Brew Barons 3–2 in front of 8,000 fans. Back in Chicago, they won a doubleheader against Kansas City, 6–5 and 9–2, knocking the Monarchs out of first place in the process.

The red-hot Atlanta Black Crackers then came home and beat Memphis 5–3 and 12–7, and moved into first place. In a Sunday doubleheader, they again swept the Red Sox, 5–4 and 8–3. Tuning up for the Monarchs, they again beat Memphis, this time in Macon, Ga., 12–6. Only Kansas City stood in the way of a second-half pennant, and the Monarchs fell 4–3 and 4–0 on consecutive days. The Atlanta Black Crackers were second-half champs, and would play Memphis for the Negro American League championship.

Over the years the Black Crackers had developed quite a rivalry with the Red Sox. "The Red Sox had an A-number-one ballclub, and we had one, and the people came there to see two ballclubs that were rivals tie up as if they were the Dodgers and New York Yankees," Kemp recalled.

149

The series had Chin Evans on the mound for the Black Crackers on September 18, 1938, in Memphis. Atlanta lost 6–1 thanks in part to the Red Sox' Neil Robinson, a second baseman who got four hits, batted in five runs, and hit two homers. Bubber "Bubbles" Brown, a pitcher signed from the Ethiopian Clowns, started for the Black Crackers in the second game, but didn't fare any better, losing 11–6. The third game was slated for a neutral site, Birmingham's Rickwood Field, but rain canceled the contest. The teams were scheduled to play a doubleheader on Sunday at Ponce de Leon Ball Park.

In between the series, the Black Crackers lost a game to the Ethiopian Clowns, an independent franchise who called themselves the best team in the country and who challenged the winner of the Atlanta-Memphis series to a Colored World Series in October.

Sportswriters around the nation loved to describe the Ethiopian Clowns. "More speed than a flock of gazelles," "the home club might just as well been facing the New York Yankees," "handling the ball with the dexterity of shell-game manipulators," "providing more fun than a three-ring circus," "ranking on a par with major league teams," and "those Clowns are the real McCoy, make no mistake about it!" were just some of the exuberant, colorful paeans.

Then, just as the series with Memphis was about to resume, the contest was abruptly canceled.

Apparently, neither team believed it could get a fair shake in the other's ballpark. The Black Crackers had lost eight straight games in Memphis, while the Red Sox had lost five in a row in Atlanta. Major R.R. Jackson, president of the Negro American League, printed this bulletin in the *Atlanta Daily World:* "Considering both sides of the Memphis-Atlanta play-off, the following decision is hereby rendered: Atlanta, for failure to report at Birmingham in time to play scheduled third game, forfeits that game to Memphis. Both teams having failed to play the required number of games to win or lose the series and as a result of disagreements and postponements of games, which both teams did not agree to as required by rules and regulations governing the Negro American League—the play-off for the championship is hereby declared *no contest.*"

Soon after, rumors flew right and left as to why the games were halted, and they're still circulating today. Some local baseball historians have speculated the two teams illegally signed players from each other and other teams, although contracts in many black baseball leagues were seldom binding, full of loopholes and rarely enforced when conflicts came up. Players were pretty much free to leave one team and sign with another if a better offer were presented.

Other theories hold that the umpires for the series were amenable to being bought off for the right amount of cash. "The umpires didn't travel with the ball clubs," Kemp said. "Only maybe the Homestead Grays or the Elites . . . or the Kansas City Monarchs . . . well, they had heavy financing and could afford to take their own public relations man and maybe sometimes a reporter and an umpire. We had to select from the people in the town, and select our umpire from them. You know just about what type of umpire you would get from a layman who didn't know the rules." In any event, no pennant was awarded for 1938, a season for which no one will ever know if the Atlanta Black Crackers might have been champions of black baseball.

Since the Black Crackers had already rented Ponce de Leon Ball Park for the anticipated doubleheader against Memphis, they invited the Birmingham Black Barons to town, and won both games. They then went south to Florida for another barnstorming trip.

THE PLAYERS MOVE ON

In 1939, the Atlanta Black Crackers franchise moved to Indianapolis and played in the Negro American League under the nickname the ABCs. And while a new Atlanta

151

Black Crackers team would later return to its roots in the Negro Southern League, many of its stars from the 1930s went on to play elsewhere.

As the ABCs' season disintegrated into disaster, Chin Evans, Pee Wee Butts, Red Moore and Bullet Dixon, along with catcher/first baseman Oscar Boone, were all sold to the Baltimore Elite Giants. After about a week in Baltimore, Evans was signed by the Newark Eagles and then finished the season with the Ethiopian Clowns. In 1940, pitching under his "clown name" of Kalihari, he was credited with a 26–4 record. But that season also provided him with his start for the Memphis Red Sox, where he remained until 1948, when he posted a 7–9 record and a 4.28 ERA. The next year he played his final season of pro ball with the Birmingham Black Barons.

After spending the rest of '39 with Baltimore, Boone signed with the Black Barons, and soon thereafter went to work for the Clowns. In 1941 he joined the Chicago-American Giants, where he shared the regular catching assignments and hitting seventh in the order when in the lineup.

During his two years with the Elites, Moore roomed with Roy Campanella while batting .248 in 1940. The next year, he joined the Army and served till the end of World War II in England, Belgium and France attached to General George Patton's legendary Third Army. He never played pro baseball again.

While in Baltimore, the 19-year-old Butts developed into the Negro National League's top shortstop. He remained in Baltimore (except for a 1943 stint in Monterey, Mexico, where he batted .248) until 1951, when he signed with Winnipeg in the Mandak League, batting .286. The next year, he played with Lincoln in the Western League but hit only .170. In 1953 he returned to the Negro American League and Birmingham and hit .240. In 1955, his last year in professional organized baseball, he hit .265 with Texas City in the Big State League.

SEMI-PROS AND COMPANY MEN

The average black baseball player made $250 a month in the 1940s, and when Lumpkin wasn't playing for the Crackers he played for company teams like the Scripto Black Cats. Organized by Sammy Haynes, the team was owned and sponsored by Scripto Manufacturing Company (Haynes managed the Black Crackers in 1946 and 1947, after joining the team in 1939 as a catcher. His career was cut short by glaucoma, and in 1969 he went totally blind.)

The Atlanta Red Caps are considered by many black baseball experts to be one of Atlanta's best semi-pro teams. The team fielded such players as Honey Williams, William Jones, Tom Craig, Carl Lippitt, Oakland Eberhardt, Walter Jones, DeWitt Pickett, Jimmy Nix, Gabby Wingfield, Robert Butts and George Linder. The team had the reputation of traveling more than any other semi-pro team in Atlanta.

Another company team was the Atlanta Steel Hooks, put together by Geech Jennings for the Atlanta Steel Plant. Some of those players included Red Moore, Glenn Mills and several other ex-collegiate stars. "We'd develop our own sandlot teams from community to community," Lumpkin recalled. "The men that ran these teams had money, a lot of which came from bootlegging. We jumped around from team to team for the money. These team owners kept up their local neighborhoods. They'd sell their liquor and then come back into the community and help the kids and the old people with money and such."

"We didn't have legal whiskey in Georgia, and these bootleggers were selling corn whiskey," Idlett said. "So the baseball teams were a front."

The Atlanta Black Crackers rejoined the Negro Southern

153

League in 1940, and Lumpkin knew and played with all of the stars of the 1940s, such as catcher Harry "Mooch" Barnes and Vinicus "Nish" Williams, of whom the *Atlanta Daily World* once wrote, "What Nish doesn't know about pitchers and how to handle them to get the best results isn't worth knowing."

Willard Brown gained later fame with Dallas of the Texas League in 1951, winning the Negro batting title, but he started with the Black Crackers during Lumpkin's tenure. "Harry 'Mooch' Barnes was another catcher of ours," Lumpkin said. "Jim Zapp, an outfielder, was a great long-ball hitter."

Outfielder Freddie Shepard played with Lumpkin. "Butch Davis played centerfield while I played left field," Lumpkin said. A kid named Othello "Chico" Renfroe hung around the team long enough that he was made a batboy, and later became "a helluva player" for the Kansas City Monarchs, Lumpkin said. After his playing career was over, Renfroe spent the rest of his days fighting for Negro League recognition as a journalist with the *Atlanta Daily World* and WIGO-AM radio.

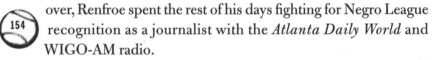

Jim "Sunny" Echols was a pitcher and center fielder with the Black Crackers, while Thomas "Monk" Flavors was a first baseman and out-fielder on the '46 team. Herschel "Bubba" Harper was a member of the 1928 semi-pro Atlanta Tigers and played with the Black Crackers until 1942.

Alfred Ingram pitched for the team from 1947 to 1951. Preston Ingram played for the 1949 Black Crackers, after spending 1940–43 with the black semi-pro Atlanta Braves and 1944–47 with the New York Black Yankees.

Mooch Barnes, also known as Tack Head, played with the Black Crackers in 1945. His career began in 1935 with the Birmingham Black Barons (1935–38), and went on to span stints with the Birmingham All-

Stars (1939–44), Chattanooga Choo Choos (1946–47), Asheville Blues (1948) and Memphis Red Sox (1949).

LIONS IN WINTER

Usually the Negro Southern League season, like its major league counterpart, ended in September, but baseball for most of these men didn't. Near the turn of the century, black Americans began going to Cuba to play baseball during the winter months. By 1910, when the Cuban leagues were firmly established, the better American players always had a Cuban option available.

In the Caribbean almost all the teams were integrated, although there were different Caribbean societies and racial traditions. American black ballplayers tested themselves against Cubans and white Americans, who also sought Latin American paychecks. The Caribbean provided the arena for the most systematic and extensive interaction by the best American ballplayers of any color.

Following Cuba's leadership, the rest of the Caribbean soon adopted baseball, and began providing opportunities for American Negro Leaguers. In the late 1930s Puerto Rico fostered a thriving baseball culture, as did the Dominican Republic for a short period in the late '30s. Panama in the '40s, along with Venezuela and Mexico, joined the large-scale world of baseball culture, contracting large numbers of black American players.

At the time baseball was integrated in 1947, black American players had the option of playing in many different Spanish-speaking countries. Not only did they earn comparatively good salaries, they also enjoyed life in non-segregated societies and played with white teammates as equals.

Ironically, the smashed color barrier also signaled the end of the Negro leagues, including the Negro Southern League

155

and the Atlanta Black Crackers. And while the Atlanta Crackers and Black Crackers never played each other, Kemp is certain which team would have prevailed if a contest had ever taken place.

"The Atlanta ball club, the white ball club, didn't have the type of outfielders I had. My outfielders I had then . . . could have gone out there and won the Southern Association pennant, 'cause all of them were hitting 15, 20, 30 and 40 home runs each. But during that time the integration of baseball had not come, so we just took it as such."

The Negro National League folded following the 1948 season and, although black teams continued to play for several years, they were no longer of major-league caliber. The demise of the Negro Leagues was inevitable as the younger black players were signed by the white major league franchises.

"There was no demand for Negro baseball as such," Billie Harden said. "They had a chance to go do better things, and this was good. Everybody was so excited over the Negroes getting a chance to go into the majors. It was beautiful. Everybody was so happy. And as Jackie went it there would be others going in. Of course, this was giving them a chance to do what they hadn't been able to do, and we were happy for it.

"So after the blacks were admitted into the majors there was no more demand for black baseball. We went on for a while, but we soon decided it would be better to let the boys go on and do better."

Indeed, few were sad to see the demise of their all-black teams, for the very existence of their leagues was nothing less than a desperate attempt to bring blacks into the mainstream of American life, liberty and the pursuit of happiness. "See, we understood the realities of segregation," Norman Lumpkin said. "We didn't like it, but we had to learn to survive with it."

HE'S SAFE!!

NINTH INNING

A NATURAL DEATH

"The Crackers' demise was a tremendous loss to Earl. Television that brought Major League Baseball into our living rooms caused him to go out of business."

—Myra Mann

Baseball was first televised on August 26, 1939, when RCA-NBC's experimental transmitter atop the Empire State Building, under the call letters W2XBS, broadcast a Brooklyn Dodgers and Cincinnati Reds doubleheader from Ebbets Field. "Television set owners as far away as 50 miles viewed the action and heard the roar of the crowd," according to the *New York Times*.

In 1951, WSB-TV was broadcasting 20 Cracker games a year. By 1954, it was televising three games a week. Radio and TV already were making baseball the national sport that it would become. Turning a knob on a little box and hearing the names of famous, beloved ballplayers . . . well, it was magical.

It also was devastating to the Southern Association and the Atlanta Crackers.

Attendance began dropping off as early as 1950, the first year a major-league game of the week was broadcast. The advent of air conditioning meant a hot, sticky, humid day at a minor-league ballpark no longer was the most enjoyable form of entertainment. Simultaneously, Little League exploded in popularity, and with two or three games a week and frequent practices, families began to stay away from minor-league stadiums more and more. Atlanta was no exception.

THE MORGAN IMAGINATION

Hank Morgan's first season covering the Crackers on radio was 1954. Born in 1917 in Atlanta, Morgan had been raised by foster parents in St. Petersburg, Fla., until his 12th birthday. Then, for the next three years, he lived in various Florida orphanages until he left and struck out on his own, never to look back.

After learning the broadcast trade in North Carolina, Morgan arrived in Atlanta where he broadcast the Wolfpack's baseball and football games. That's where he learned to recreate out-of-town games from Western Union wires. After a stint in Jacksonville, he came to Atlanta on WQXI, 790 on your AM dial.

"Recreating games was fun because you could use your imagination," Morgan said. "When broadcasting the Cracker road trips, I stayed about a half-inning behind. I had a dial that recreated general crowd noise, and when there'd been a hit, I'd crack a small wooden bat on a nearby billy club, and generate the cheering sound by turning another dial. You could let your imagination run wild.

"Broadcasting a live game was entirely different, because not only did you have to call the game, but I also kept up my own records, such as batting averages, ledgers and scoring. Today, broadcasters have piles and piles of information from teams' sports information people."

The radio booth at Ponce was big enough . . . for a radio booth. "On the television side, we had an oversized broom closet that was a little more plush than the radio guys had," said long-time Atlanta broadcast journalist Ray Moore.

FROM WORST TO FIRST

The Crackers of '55 suffered through an awful season, finishing seventh with a record of 70–84 (.455). The team started out under the guidance of George McQuinn, who left during the season to be replaced by Clyde King. The season was unremarkable in every way, except the fact that Atlanta again led the league in attendance with 239,037 passing through the turnstiles.

Crackers outfielder Jack Daniels in 1956. *Tracey O'Neal Collection, Pullen Library, Georgia State University.*

Then came the beginning of a two-year stretch in which the Crackers would dominate like the days of old.

Clyde King was a devout Christian who abhorred four-letter words. "When an umpire made a call that Clyde disagreed with, he'd run over to the umpire, yell and scream, thrown his cap in the dirt, jump up and down, and generally pitch a fit," Morgan said. "But Clyde never said a cuss word, ever.

"Well, Billy 'Ace' Reynolds, who was a Cracker outfielder, was sitting in the dugout during one game, and Clyde was

The scoreboard at Poncey, circa 1955.
Tracey O'Neal Collection, Pullen Library, Georgia State University.

out there at first base arguing with an umpire. Billy leaned over to his teammates and said, 'Skipper's really cussing out that umpire.' And one of the other Crackers said, 'Oh no, Billy, [King] never cusses.'

"Billy, of course, didn't believe it. So he walked out near first base, searching the ground with his eyes, acting as if he's looking for something. But all the while, he's listening. So when he goes back to the dugout, his teammates asked him, 'What's the skipper saying to that umpire?' And Billy says, 'Oh, it's terrible. I've never heard anything like it. He's saying, "Golly, gosh darn, gee whillikers, how could you make a call like that?"'"

Morgan also recalled another particularly bizarre tale. One of Poncey's walls supported a sign in the form of a giant three-dimensional Coca-Cola bottle, complete with a hard rubber cap on top.

"A player from a visiting team hit a long ball that struck that rubber cap so hard that it knocked the cap off, and then the ball fell into the Coke bottle," Morgan said. "Reynolds was running all over the outfield, yelling, 'Where's the ball? Where's the ball?'"

Outfielder Jack Daniels was the leadoff man for the '56 Crackers. "He was the most unusual leadoff hitter I ever saw," Morgan said. "Every time at bat either resulted in a home run, a walk or a strikeout, it seemed. He hit 34 home runs, walked 143 times and struck out 113 times that year. He scored 126 runs and led the club in everything. In his 669 times at bat, he reached base 320 times, counting walks and hits, and that's nearly a .500 average."

In 1956, Corky Valentine was the third-highest-rated pitcher in the league, with a 16–7 record and a 3.89 ERA. Clarence Riddle held down first base, Frank DiPrima had the best hitting average among second basemen (.298), and Sam Meeks was a utilityman.

The Crackers also were the team strikeout champions of the league, with 815. The team posted its 15th pennant with a record of 89–65 (.578), and swept four games from the Barons before whipping the Chicks over a full seven–game set in the playoffs. But Houston went on to defeat the Crackers in the Dixie Series, four games to two.

A HERO FROM THE PAST

Mann's old outfielder Buddy Bates returned to manage the Crackers to a 16th pennant in 1957, the last year the Southern Association would draw more than one million paid admissions throughout. Atlanta itself drew 256,000.

Bates had been a star player for the Crackers in '40 and '41, and called the '41 team the "best I ever played with." Mann called his new manager "the greatest centerfielder I ever saw in any league."

161

"He was such a fine judge of fly balls that he'd turn his back to the diamond and go racing up the centerfield bank, or off toward a corner, and be camped on the spot when the ball came down," Mann said at the time of Bates' hiring. "He made every play look easy, except one. Gus Dugas of Nashville hit a tremendous smash over the little centerfield fence that runs from the signboards to the flagpole. Buddy went up the bank like a mountain goat, leaned back over the fence and speared the drive with one hand.

"In all my years at Ponce de Leon, that's the only home-run ball I have seen caught over the centerfield fence."

NO ACTS OF MERCY, PLEASE

World War II had interrupted Bates' playing career, but not before his most embarrassing moment came in a freak accident never before or since seen in a professional baseball game.

Bates was in the minors, playing in Toronto. At the Blue Jays playing field, a light pole just outside the foul line was steadied by a guy wire stretched down along the rightfield fence. Rightfielder and teammate Johnny Seeds jumped high up against the fence in a vain attempt to grab at a ball hit over his head. The ball bounced back into the field, but Seeds' leg caught in the wire, leaving the poor fellow hanging there upside down.

"It looked as if his leg might be broken," Bates later recalled. "I got him untangled and on his feet, and discovered he was only skinned up a little. Meanwhile, the runner had circled the bases for a home run. When I went back to the dugout the manager gave me the worst dressing down of my lifetime.

"Before he finished I realized I had been hired as a ballplayer and not a first-aider, and I was supposed to throw the ball in before I performed any acts of mercy."

In 1957, Atlanta set a new league record for team base-on-balls with

754, breaking Mobile's previous record of 752 in 1948. And for the second straight year, they were the team strikeout champions of the league, with 797. Again Riddle held down first, while DiPrima batted .281. A solid one-two-three punch was provided by a trio of starter-relievers: right-hander Don Nottebart (18–10, 46G, 25 GS), southpaw Ken McKenzie (a very intelligent hurler who Casey Stengel would later call his "Yalie" and who posted a record

1957 Atlanta Crackers replica cap.

of 14–6, 43 G, 27 GS) and leftie Jack O'Donnell (16–10, 59 G, 13 GS) who won four decisions in four days against the Mobile Bears.

This time Atlanta, which finished the season with an 87–67 (.565) record, swept four games against Memphis in the playoffs to win the Shaughnessy, only after they put away the Lookouts in the first round, four games to two. But again they lost to Houston in the Dixie, four games to two.

Thus ended the glory days of Earl Mann's Atlanta Crackers in the Southern Association. Bates returned to guide the club in 1958, posting a 84–70 (.545) record, enough to finish in third place. But in the Shaughnessy playoffs they were swept by Mobile, enough to ensure Bates' ouster. Mann hired the all-time Cracker home-run leader, Bob Montag, to guide the 1959 club. Only 17,000 people would pass through Poncey's gates as the Crackers finished dead last in the league at 56–96 (.368).

THE END OF THE LINE

All the while, Mann, like the rest of the league owners, was losing money badly, so he began looking for a potential

163

buyer of the team. Two young Chicago lawyers visited him, Jack Shaffer and William Chatz, who represented a wealthy client also based in Chicago. This anonymous buyer wanted to bring the Crackers into the newly founded Continental League. For reasons only he knew, Mann refused their offer.

On November 4, 1959, Mann turned over the Atlanta Cracker franchise to the Southern Association. Walter O'Malley bought it for the Dodgers, marking the first time that a major league club operated the Crackers outright. Until L.A. came to bat, the Milwaukee Braves appeared to be the only big-league operation willing to look at the Atlanta market. But despite the working agreement between the Braves and Atlanta that dated back to 1950, Milwaukee management backed out in the middle of the negotiations.

Southern Association president Charlie Hurth and Dodgers vice president Buzzie Bauasi sealed the deal that brought the Dodgers to Atlanta; their meeting took place at the Vinoy Park Hotel in St. Petersburg, Fla.

164

"We think Atlanta is a great baseball town, and the game can't afford to lose such a franchise," Bausai said at the time. "We want to help the Southern Association." By then, however, the league was beyond any cure at all.

"A TREMENDOUS LOSS"

"The Crackers' demise was a tremendous loss to Earl," said Mann's widow, Myra. "Television that brought Major League Baseball into our living rooms caused him to go out of business, but it also allowed him to help bring the Braves to Atlanta. He was there when Atlanta Stadium broke ground."

Plans for the sale of Poncey and a new stadium actually had begun in the late 1950s, "plans that will please some baseball fans and bring distress to others," according to the *Atlanta Journal* on January 30, 1959. "The sentimental, with cherished memories of exciting afternoons and evenings at Poncey, will find it difficult to envisage the Crackers in another setting. Those who go along with demands for change hope for a glittering new stadium, better parking facilities and perhaps a move to a league of higher classification.

"Ponce de Leon has served long and well. The grandstand is growing old, but it was soundly constructed and viewing conditions are good. When the lights come on at dusk the playing area makes a most attractive picture. Across the nation are scores of fields not nearly as comfortable and inviting as Ponce, but times have changed, and the property has become too valuable for further use in baseball."

The city's population was changing along with the times, and Atlanta was becoming a different place to live and work. As the population grew, so did the number of Northerners and Midwesterners who came to settle in the city. These new Atlantans preferred to spend their recreational time at venues other than an ancient baseball field. Golf and tennis became more popular, lakes Lanier and Allatoona were built, and Georgia Tech's Grant Field was expanded to seat more Ramblin' Wreck fans. Paul Jones, a promotional genius if there ever was one, began staging professional wrestling matches at the new Atlanta Municipal Auditorium, and the $2-million Atlanta International Raceway was built in nearby Hampton, Ga., in 1960.

The Crackers attendance began to decline even more. Too bad, because a lot of people missed out on really fine baseball.

A NEW BEGINNING . . . IF ONLY FOR A WHILE

The Crackers would play until 1961 in the Southern Association, winning an all-time record 17th pennant by only a half-game in 1960. The presence of the Dodgers gave the franchise one of its most exciting and promising young teams ever, yet only 154,000 people went to Poncey during the '60 season.

Managed by Rube Walker, one of the team's best single perform-ances came from 20-year-old Pete Richert, a pitcher who won 19 games and broke the Pelicans' Goat Walker's 40-year-old strikeout record with 251 in 136 innings.

Atlanta held a commanding first-place lead in August but went into a tailspin which climaxed with doubleheader losses to Mobile on the last two days of the season, September 10 and 11. In the meantime, the new Shreveport Sports became almost unbeatable under catcher/manager Les Peden. Shreveport ended its season on September 11 with a doubleheader in Nashville, winning the opening game for their 25th victory in 28 games. A win in the nightcap would have given the Sports the pennant, and they led 1–0 heading into the eighth. But the Vols rallied to tie the game, then won it in the ninth, 2–1, which handed Atlanta the league title. The Crackers, though, never made it through the first round of the Shaughnessies, as they were upended by the fourth-place Birmingham Barons.

The Southern Association gasped its last breath in 1961, thus ending minor league baseball's most storied organization. Both New Orleans and Memphis, long-time mainstays in the league, had lost their franchises in the offseason, every remaining team was losing money, and an all-time low 59,000 people visited Ponce de Leon Ball Park. The Southern Association thus dismantled after 61 seasons of play.

The Crackers would live on for a few more years under new owners and in a new league. In 1962, Joe Ryan, owner of a St. Louis Cardinals' AAA International franchise in Charleston, W.Va., wanted to move his team to Atlanta. The deal almost fell apart, though, because of an old feud between Ryan and Mann, who was still the owner of Poncey. Fortunately, arrangements were finally made that would allow the

Crackers to live on in a league with as much history as the old Southern Association.

THE INTERNATIONAL LEAGUE
BRINGS TRIPLE-A TO TOWN

The International League was formed from three leagues—the Eastern, founded in 1884; the New York State League, formed in 1885; and the Ontario League, organized also in 1885. The New York State and Ontario loops merged in 1886 to form the International League. Final consolidation of the three units took place in 1887 when the Eastern was absorbed by the International to form a 10-city circuit.

But the league wasn't very successful. The Northern clubs, arguing that the Southerns were too far away, withdrew from the circuit (which promptly collapsed) and reorganized themselves as the International Association.

In 1890 major-league players had organized their own Players' (Brotherhood) League in competition with the National and American associations. Bidding for players by the three leagues led to skyrocketing salaries. The league folded on July 7, the only time the International ever disbanded before season's end.

Charles D. White reorganized the International in 1891 as the Eastern Association. Its name was changed to Eastern League in 1892, and only six clubs of eight players each could finish the season. In 1893 Pat Powers began a 17-year tenure of office as International president. He served until 1911, his reign interrupted by a one-year term in 1906 for Harry L. Taylor of Buffalo, later a justice of the New York State Supreme Court. Under Powers, the International would become an institution.

In 1903, a long, tranquil and prosperous era had begun and the International League membership remained

167

unchanged for 11 years. Baseball flourished across the country as never before, as new International League stadiums were built with the support of trolley-car companies, just as in the Crackers' early days before the turn of the century.

For the International, however, that era came to an end when Pat Powers relinquished the presidency to Ed Barrow, as national baseball's prosperity spelled trouble for the International.

In 1914 the Federal League was organized by a group of wealthy men who decided the time was ripe for another major baseball loop. They decided the best way to accumulate franchises was to adopt a strategy similar to Kaiser Germany's expansionist policy of gobbling up smaller, poorly defended neighbors. So three International cities were invaded: Baltimore and Buffalo in 1914 and Newark in 1915, thus earning the International the sympathetic title of "the Belgium of baseball."

Barrow received assurance that if the older, more established leagues won this latest power play, he would head a new major league. It was not to be. The great baseball war ended as others have, in compromise and consolidation. The Baltimore Feds alone were dissatisfied with the results of the deal and carried their battle into the U.S. Supreme Court. Justice Oliver Wendell Holmes wrote in the majority opinion in *Federal Baseball Club v. National and American League* (1922) that the game was not subject to federal antitrust laws because a team's "business is giving exhibitions of baseball, which are purely state affairs" rather than interstate commerce. This exemption continues to shield present-day teams owners, despite the television contracts, merchandise licensing, and stadium deals of the $3.5-billion industry, from being sued as a monopoly and gives them the power to control the movement of franchises.

World War I brought in its wake another crisis for the International. Attendance fell and club finances barely made it through the war.

Financially feeble, the league was compelled to reorganize as the New International in 1918. Barrow, his salary halved, stepped down. In this hectic war year the International, alone of all the minors, completed its season, while it searched for financially sound cities.

Franchise cities changed regularly until 1936, and from 1937–1949, the International League enjoyed its longest period without change. Afterward, the advent of TV saw the collapse of some clubs and the replacement of others. A new era began with the admission of Havana, Cuba, in 1954. The league, now truly international, embraced three countries. But in 1960, with Fidel Castro's ascendancy and the nationalization of foreign industry in Cuba, the league transferred its Havana franchise to Jersey City, N.J., in midseason.

A NEW DAY FILLED WITH OLD ENEMIES

The minor leagues' battle to neutralize the effects of TV still was being fought in the 1960s when the league expanded into Atlanta. So the Crackers, despite a new owner and new players in a new league, were still to be plagued by their old enemies.

Joe Schultz took the Crackers' reins in 1962 after a stint with the Charleston Marlins, who he had led to a second-place finish in 1961. Schultz had started his baseball career in 1936 in Albany, Ga., as a catcher. He was with the St. Louis Browns from 1943–1949, and was one of the American League's best pinch hitters. In 1946 Schultz batted .386 as a pinch hitter and spot catcher. He enjoyed phenomenal success against the Cleveland Indians, with a lifetime batting average of .410, and even hit Hall of Famer Bob Feller pretty hard.

Schultz began managing at Wichita in 1950, then moved on to stints in Tulsa, Nashville, San Antonio, York, Omaha and Memphis. He knew Atlanta very well before taking over the Crackers, having managed Nashville in 1955 and Memphis in 1960.

169

The '62 season under Schultz marked the first time an integrated Cracker team took the field. Playing in the International with the Jacksonville Suns, Toronto Maple Leafs, Rochester Red Wings, Columbus Jets, Buffalo Bisons, Richmond Virginians and Syracuse Chiefs, Atlanta saw two six-game winning streaks, but lost seven straight during May. Twice, they scored 12 runs, their most of the season, against Richmond on June 6 and against Syracuse on June 22.

On May 17, the club hit six home runs against Rochester, and outfielder Robert Burda hit three himself on August 1 against Buffalo. Burda struck again on August 11, when he scored five hits against Syracuse. Another outfielder, John Glenn, equaled Burda's mark on September 1 against Jacksonville, when he connected with five balls in one game.

Righthander John Kucks won eight consecutive games, and led the team in victories with 14. Grover Leroy "Lefty" Gregory lost five straight at one point. Harry Fanok, a switch-hitting righthander, racked up 14 strikeouts on July 3 against Columbus, and finished the year with 192. Another righthander, Bob Sadowski, led the team in shutouts, with two.

Burda was Atlanta's top hitter with a .303 batting average and 74 RBIs. Second sacker Phil Gagliano led the team with 158 hits, 30 doubles and 87 runs. Infielder Joseph Morgan, Glenn and outfielder James Beauchamp—a football, basketball, track and baseball star in high school—tied for the team lead in triples, four. Morgan also led the team in 76 base-on-balls, while outfielder Michael Shannon stole five bases during the season. Infielder Fred Whitfield batted safely in 17 games. Gagliano made the '62 International League all-star team, the only Cracker so honored.

"WE WERE CRACKERS"

Also on the Crackers roster that year was a catcher who had spent the previous season in San Juan, Charleston and Memphis. A 1962 press handbook describes the 22-year-old Memphis native as an "all-around athlete. Captain of baseball and football teams at Christian Brothers High School. Star basketball player. All-Star team—Midwest League, 1959." His name? James Timothy McCarver.

Tim McCarver roomed with Gagliano, another Memphis native, and Sadowski. "[Sadowski] was like a brother to me," McCarver said. "And we were Crackers! I had a brand new '61 blue Grand Prix, and many nights we'd drive to this little oyster bar nearby, and consume unbelievable amounts of Boston clam chowder, po' boy sandwiches and oysters. We couldn't get enough food.

"Atlanta was in a very innocent stage of its history back then."

Not so innocent was a particularly vicious fight that took place early in the season between Atlanta and the visiting Maple Leafs. "They came into town and just destroyed us," McCarver recalled. "The last two games were a doubleheader, and the score was something like 16–1. Lou Jackson, one of their outfielders, was on second base and was trying to steal third, but Lou Vickery, our pitcher, brought him back to second.

"Joe Schultz told Lou that if the S.O.B. tried to steal another base, he was to hit the batter. So the next time it happened, Lou hit the batter, and that's when both benches emptied." McCarver and Toronto's Bill Lajoie (later to become general manager of the Detroit Tigers) were fighting, and Toronto second baseman George "Sparky" Anderson "was nearly killed by Burda," McCarver said. "The whole thing was really nasty."

In late August the team heard that Cardinal management was going to fire Schultz from the organization completely after the season. "He was like a father to me," McCarver said. "I'd have done anything for Joe Schultz." Atlanta staged a furious late-season charge toward the pennant that culminated in the third-best records at home and on the road, 41–36 and 42–35 respectively, and an overall record of 83–71, to finish fourth.

171

WIN IT FOR JOE

On a roll, the Crackers whipped first-place Jacksonville in round one of the playoffs, while the second-place Maple Leafs bested third-place Columbus, thus setting the stage for the Junior World Series.

"During the '62 season, we had an unbelievable number of rain-outs, and because of them, we wound up having to play Toronto in a doubleheader at the end of September to decide the championship," McCarver said. "We all wanted to win the series for Joe, and it was a tremendously emotional experience."

The Crackers did win it for Joe, with Ray Sadecki on the mound in the first game and Gregory going all nine innings for the second, as both games were decided by a score of 2–1. The Atlanta Crackers were minor-league baseball champions for the last time.

"Miracle is the word for it," the *Atlanta Constitution* said when the Crackers won the Junior World Series. "The astounding Atlanta Crackers staged a brilliant late-summer drive that won them the Junior World Series. Seldom, we venture to say, has a minor-league team gone so far so fast. The 1962 Crackers have earned themselves a niche in baseball history."

And so impressed was Cardinal management with the performance of Schultz's team that they rehired him as a major-league coach for the '63 season! That led the way for Harry Walker to assume the managerial helm for the 1963 season, leading the Crackers, still under Cardinal management, to an 85–68 record but no league championship, as the team never made it through round one of the playoffs. The '63 season was also the first in which the International League reorganized, albeit for only a year, into two divisions, Northern and Southern. William B. McKechnie Jr. served as team president, with Dick King vice president.

Minor-league ball was played on this site on Ponce de Leon Avenue (shown circa 1962), first as R.J. Spiller Field (1907–23), and later as Ponce de Leon Ball Park (1924–65). After 57 years of play, the site was razed for a strip mall.

IN COME THE TWINS

The Cardinals relinquished their ties to Atlanta after that season, and in came the Minnesota Twins to field a AAA team, still in the International League. The Crackers finished dead last in the league in '64, a dreadful 55–93, despite Sandy Valdespino batting .337 to lead the league. Jack McKeon was manager.

By 1965 the whole world knew the Milwaukee Braves were heading south, and the Crackers played as the Braves' AAA farm team in the brand spanking new Atlanta Stadium. Tommie Aaron hit the very first home run in a place soon to be dubbed "the launching pad."

Also getting his start in Atlanta around that time was the son of Harry Carey, the legendary caller of the Chicago Cubs.

173

"We were at the Houston Astrodome in 1965, and Mel Allen and I were supposed to call a Milwaukee Braves game," Hank Morgan recalled. "Mel's mother had recently died, and we all knew Mel wouldn't make the game. Ernie Johnson had just joined us as a rookie broadcaster, and he and I were going to call the Braves game on the television side. Johnson asked me about the radio side for the game, and I suggested flying Skip Carey out there to call the game. He was calling the Cracker games on radio, but I knew he wouldn't mind missing one of those to call a major-league game."

As the last minor-league baseball team in Atlanta history, the Crackers finished a second-place 83–64 under skipper Bill Adair. They lost to Toronto in round one of the playoffs, four games to one.

Before the Braves officially came, McKechnie tried to sell the franchise territory to the Atlanta Stadium Authority, which had been formed to oversee the construction of the new Atlanta Stadium. His asking price was $300,000, and the authority offered $250,000; both figures were extraordinarily high for a dying organization.

Pleading with the board, McKechnie said, "Gentlemen, we're talking about one of the greatest franchises in minor-league baseball."

THE BRAVES ARRIVE

But it wasn't to be. The ink already had dried on the contract that would bring the Milwaukee Braves to the southland. The Atlanta Braves were newly christened, and the city joyfully replaced the hopefulness embodied by the minor leagues with the cold and selfish financial realities of the majors, realities made all the harsher today.

So ended the remarkable adventures of the Atlanta Crackers, one of the finest minor-league baseball teams of all time. From their beginnings in 1901 to their last season in 1965, they won more league championships than any other team in all of organized baseball, save the New York Yankees. And like the city they called home, the Atlanta Crackers represented an era that was far simpler and more innocent than the times in which we live today.

Now, in an age in which salaries, contract disputes, and players' on- and off-field antics sometimes cross the border of the offensive into the realm of the absurd, we wonder where our innocence has been lost—and how we might get it back.

EXTRA INNING

THE LAST SENTINEL

"We let Earl Mann die and didn't do anything about it."

—Stephen Schmidt

I n 1967, Earl and Myra Mann married. At the time, he was repre-
senting the Coca-Cola Co. in various sports promotional capacities
and assignments. Three years later, the couple moved to Palm
Beach, Fla.

Mann continued attending the Olympic games every four years,
even after the couple opened a successful real estate practice. He
became a regular fixture at Atlanta Braves' spring training camps.
Chuck Tanner, who later would manage the Braves, called him "the
man who was most responsible for all of the fortunate things that have
happened to me in my career."

In the late 1980s, Mann began suffering from a series of ailments.
First, a fractured hip had to be replaced. It dislocated, and was
replaced again, and replaced yet again after a second dislocation.

Mann would never again stand on his feet after the third replacement, and spent the last three years of his life bedridden.

On January 4, 1990, after a bout with pneumonia, Earl Mann died. He was 84. The body was cremated, and the ashes spread underneath the giant magnolia, the last sentinel guarding the remains of Ponce de Leon Ball Park.

Three years later, on May 8, 1993, Stephen Schmidt, a longtime Cracker fan and close friend of Mann, and several other longtime Cracker players and faithful organized a tribute to Mann under the cool shade of the old magnolia tree.

Schmidt, whose company, Dixie Seal & Stamp, manufactures license plates for the frontages of automobiles, made red, white and blue commemorative Atlanta Cracker plates to be given to the first 300 people in attendance. Incredibly, more than 800 showed up, "so many of them wearing their Cracker hats and uniforms," said Myra Mann. "It was incredibly touching. Earl would have been so proud that his town [was] going to be the host for the Olympics."

In attendance, besides Schmidt and Mrs. Mann, were Oreon Mann and Bob Montag. Bishop Bevel Jones delivered the eulogy, and Hank Morgan recalled Mann's life in baseball. During the ceremony, Schmidt displayed a plaque to the audience that read

EARL MANN

1904–1990

"MR. ATLANTA BASEBALL"

1933–1959

RIVERDALE, GEORGIA, FARM BOY

ATLANTA TECH HIGH GRADUATE

OGLETHORPE UNIVERSITY STUDENT

BUILDER OF A BASEBALL DYNASTY

**HERE ON THESE GROUNDS AT
PONCE DE LEON BALL PARK,
HE ROSE FROM PEANUT VENDOR IN 1916,
TO GENERAL MANAGER IN 1933,
TO PRESIDENT IN 1935, TO OWNER IN 1949
OF THE ATLANTA CRACKERS BASEBALL TEAM.**

**MANN FASHIONED THE CLUB INTO A MODEL FOR
MINOR LEAGUE TEAMS.
HE PRODUCED TEN PENNANT WINNERS, KNOWN AS
"THE YANKEES OF THE MINORS."**

**HE FURNISHED MORE PLAYERS FOR THE MAJORS THAN
ANY OTHER OPERATOR OF HIS ERA. HE LED ATLANTA
IN BECOMING A MAJOR LEAGUE CITY. HE WAS
INSTRUMENTAL IN BRINGING THE BRAVES TO ATLANTA.**

Earlier, Schmidt asked for permission to erect the plaque under the magnolia tree, where Mann's ashes had been scattered. The owners of Ponce Square, the site of the former Ponce de Leon Ball Park, refused the request.

179

AFTERWORD

My dad was fifteen when he left home to seek his fortune. One more year at Albany High and he would have had a football scholarship to the University of Georgia, but like many kids of the Great Depression, he couldn't wait. He ended up a journeyman minor-league baseball player who also managed to serve during two wars—Korea and Vietnam—between baseball assignments in places such as Montreal, Fort Worth, Mobile, and Atlanta.

Once, he got the golden call—the Brooklyn Dodgers! He phoned home before boarding a train in Kansas City. He was getting pretty old. This was his last and only chance—but he was ready! Two days later he arrived in Brooklyn and realized his dream: he donned a white flannel uniform with *Brooklyn Dodgers* scripted across the chest. He told me he scorched the ball during batting practice and Charlie Dressen told him he'd be catching the next afternoon. It didn't happen. The Dodgers were in a tight race and my dad was merely insurance if a big trade couldn't be made.

The follow-up call came about two A.M. My dad admitted he thought it was a cruel joke at first, but soon realized it was Dressen on the line—and serious. They'd made a trade with Atlanta for another catcher. The next day dad was back on a train, heading south.

At the time it wasn't all that bad to be an Atlanta Cracker. The pay was great (indeed, some of the players made more than some major leaguers) and if you were from the South, anyway, it was almost like being a big leaguer.

Atlanta was a teeming baseball city and the life was good. I was young, but I remember that every night was a sellout and I think we won every home game and the players were treated like royalty anywhere near old Ponce de Leon Ball Park. My mother was pretty and my dad was handsome and he could hit and throw and life was beautiful. I got to play catch with the players—some nights out in front of the dugout, even after the lights came on. When I'd join my mother and sister in the stands, people would come up and jokingly ask for my autograph. There was no doubt in my young mind about my destiny.

But a five-year-old could only see the excitement and the beauty: the multi-tiered fences in front of the railroad tracks where, in later years, Bob Montag would drive the ball far into the night; or where Chuck Tanner would climb the fence like Spiderman to rob the opposing hitters of many extra-base hits; or the magnificent magnolia high up on the magnificent knoll in center which legendary Hall of Famer Eddie Mathews would bombard with gigantic home runs about once a week.

And the smell of the popcorn, the fantastic cool thrill of a bottled Coke fresh off the ice, and the feeling of pride as we waited for Dad outside the locker room on humid summer nights. Then the walk home. (Yes, we lived *that* close to the ballpark.) As a family, we'd sit on the screened porch of our apartment and maybe enjoy a midnight snack as we listened to Dad as he went over the game and wound down. On some nights my parents let me sleep on the screened porch and I'd go to sleep with the glow of the lights from Ponce de Leon Park on my face. I can still hear the late-night traffic on Ponce de Leon Avenue and if I woke in the night, and the lights from the ballpark had been cut off, I was still not alone. The neon-red Sears, Roebuck sign across Ponce still cast a comforting light on the ballpark—the ballpark where I thought my dad would play forever.

But I was only five, almost six, and I could only see the excitement and the beauty. I didn't know about war, racism, divorce, finances, or loneliness. God shelters the very young and the very old. And now I have been both.

My dad got drafted. And our lives changed. In time, my mother and father divorced and I ended up living in southwest Georgia with my grandparents, while my mother and sister moved back to my mother's hometown of Clinton, Iowa, where my dad had met her in the first place, while playing there.

In the fifties, while I was at Georgia Tech, my teammates and I would often attend games at Ponce de Leon Park. The Crackers were AA then, still winning almost every game and, to tell you the truth, it was the most exciting place to watch a game I've ever known.

Once in a while, my buddies would look over and see me sitting there crying and rib me a little bit. But that was okay. They just didn't understand. We weren't watching the same game.

BOBBY DEWS
Alanta Braves

"One reason I have always loved baseball so much is that it has been
not merely "the great national game," but really a part
of the whole weather of our lives, of the thing that is our own,
of the whole fabric, the million memories of America."

—Thomas Wolfe

Old-Timers Game at Atlanta-Fulton County Stadium, 1975
(Front row, left to right) James "Red" Moore, P.I. Butts;
(back row, left to right) Roy Hawkins, Jim Greene, Cecil Travis.

APPENDICES POST-GAME WRAP-UP

Atlanta Minor League Baseball Regular Season Records: 1885–1965

1885		
Atlanta	60–31	.659
Augusta	68–36	.653
Macon	58–48	.547
Columbus	42–39	.518
Nashville	55–37	.507
Memphis	38–54	.413
Chattanooga	30–59	.337
Birmingham	17–64	.210

1886		
Atlanta	64–28	.695
Savannah	56–33	.629
Nashville	46–43	.517
Memphis	44–46	.488
Charleston	41–50	.450
Augusta	21–31	.404
Macon	32–59	.351
Chattanooga	20–34	.270

1887		
New Orleans	75–40	.652
Charleston	65–41	.613
Memphis	64–52	.551
Nashville	34–30	.531
Birmingham	20–61	.246
Mobile	5–19	.208
Savannah	7–27	.205

1888		
Birmingham	32–19	.627
Memphis	26–24	.520
New Orleans	25–32	.438
Charleston	20–28	.416

1889		
New Orleans	43–7	.860
Charleston	22–14	.611
Atlanta	19–25	.479
Memphis	12–24	.333
Mobile	6–17	.261
Birmingham	4–17	.190

1892		
Birmingham	73–50	.593
Mobile	66–57	.537
New Orleans	66–57	.537
Montgomery	66–58	.532
Chattanooga	63–57	.525
Atlanta	58–65	.472
Macon	51–69	.425
Memphis	46–76	.377

1893		
Charleston	51–32	.614
Macon	54–38	.587
Atlanta	55–39	.585
Memphis	53–38	.581
Savannah	53–38	.581
Augusta	51–39	.567
Chattanooga	48–45	.516
New Orleans	40–51	.439
Mobile	38–53	.417
Montgomery	38–57	.400
Birmingham	25–39	.391
Nashville	33–60	.355
Pensacola	9–19	.321

1894		
Memphis	39–17	.702
Mobile	38–19	.655
Charleston	33–22	.600
Savannah	30–26	.536
New Orleans	28–33	.468
Nashville	24–33	.414
Atlanta	21–37	.362
Macon	15–41	.268

1895		
Atlanta	70–37	.654
Nashville	69–38	.645
Evansville	66–38	.635
Memphis	32–37	.464
Mobile	37–63	.455
Montgomery	40–70	.364

1896		
New Orleans	68–31	.686
Montgomery	60–36	.625
Atlanta	36–36	.500
Mobile	39–56	.410
Birmingham	26–41	.388
Columbus	34–63	.350

1899		
Mobile	24–10	.600
Shreveport	20–21	.488
New Orleans	20–22	.476
Dallas	17–22	.430
Montgomery	4–9	.308

1901		
Nashville	80–40	.634
Little Rock	76–45	.628
Memphis	68–55	.610
New Orleans	68–55	.584
Shreveport	55–66	.455
Chattanooga	45–73	.391
Birmingham	45–70	.390
Selma	37–78	.322

1902		
Nashville	80–40	.667
Little Rock	77–45	.611
New Orleans	72–47	.605
Atlanta	55–63	.605
Chattanooga	50–68	.424
Shreveport	48–72	.400
Birmingham	39–80	.327

1903		
Memphis	73–51	.589
Little Rock	71–50	.587
Shreveport	68–58	.539
Atlanta	62–60	.508
Nashville	60–64	.484
Birmingham	59–64	.480
Montgomery	53–67	.442
New Orleans	46–78	.370

1904		
Memphis	81–54	.600
Atlanta	78–57	.578
New Orleans	79–58	.577
Birmingham	73–64	.533
Nashville	72–67	.518
Little Rock	61–74	.452
Shreveport	55–81	.404
Montgomery	44–88	.333

1905		
New Orleans	84–45	.651
Montgomery	73–54	.575
Atlanta	71–61	.542
Shreveport	69–60	.535
Birmingham	70–61	.534
Memphis	69–62	.527
Nashville	47–88	.348
Little Rock	37–90	.291

1906		
Birmingham	86–46	.652
Memphis	79–55	.590
Atlanta	80–56	.588
New Orleans	75–61	.551
Shreveport	70–66	.588
Montgomery	64–65	.496
Nashville	45–92	.328
Little Rock	40–98	.290

1907		
Atlanta	78–54	.591
Memphis	74–57	.565
New Orleans	68–66	.507
Little Rock	66–66	.500
Birmingham	61–71	.474
Shreveport	62–70	.470
Montgomery	62–71	.466
Nashville	59–78	.431

1908		
Nashville	75–56	.573
New Orleans	76–57	.571
Memphis	73–62	.540
Montgomery	68–65	.511
Mobile	67–67	.500
Atlanta	63–72	.467
Little Rock	62–76	.449
Birmingham	53–82	.333

1909		
Atlanta	87–49	.640
Nashville	82–55	.594
Montgomery	76–60	.559
New Orleans	73–64	.533
Mobile	67–77	.454
Birmingham	60–79	.429
Little Rock	59–80	.424
Memphis	51–88	.367

1910		
New Orleans	87–53	.621
Birmingham	79–61	.564
Atlanta	75–63	.543
Chattanooga	66–71	.482
Nashville	64–76	.457
Mobile	63–75	.457
Memphis	62–76	.449
Montgomery	59–80	.421

1911		
New Orleans	78–54	.591
Montgomery	77–58	.570
Birmingham	76–62	.551
Nashville	69–64	.519
Chattanooga	67–71	.486
Memphis	62–71	.466
Mobile	57–76	.429
Atlanta	54–84	.391

1912		
Birmingham	89–51	.625
Mobile	79–58	.576
New Orleans	71–64	.526
Nashville	67–70	.489
Memphis	68–71	.489
Montgomery	64–75	.460
Chattanooga	59–75	.440
Atlanta	54–83	.394

1913		
Atlanta	81–56	.591
Mobile	81–57	.587
Birmingham	74–64	.536
Chattanooga	70–64	.526
Montgomery	68–69	.496
Memphis	64–74	.463
Nashville	62–76	.446
New Orleans	45–85	.346

1914		
Birmingham	88–62	.587
Mobile	88–67	.562
New Orleans	80–65	.552
Atlanta	78–66	.542
Nashville	77–72	.542
Chattanooga	73–78	.483
Memphis	61–78	.412
Montgomery	54–100	.351

1915		
New Orleans	91–63	.591
Birmingham	86–67	.562
Memphis	81–73	.526
Nashville	75–78	.490
Atlanta	74–79	.483
Chattanooga	73–78	.476
Mobile	68–86	.441
Little Rock	65–87	.427

1916		
Nashville	84–54	.609
New Orleans	73–61	.544
Birmingham	87–66	.526
Little Rock	70–65	.518
Atlanta	70–67	.511
Memphis	68–70	.493
Chattanooga	65–74	.467
Mobile	45–91	.331

1917		
Atlanta	98–56	.637
New Orleans	89–61	.593
Birmingham	87–66	.569
Memphis	81–73	.569
Nashville	77–73	.513
Chattanooga	76–74	.507
Little Rock	64–86	.427
Mobile	34–117	.220

1918		
New Orleans	49–21	.700
Little Rock	41–28	.594
Mobile	35–32	.522
Birmingham	33–31	.516
Chattanooga	35–34	.507
Memphis	32–28	.457
Nashville	30–40	.429
Atlanta	18–49	.269

1919		
Atlanta	85–53	.616
Little Rock	74–56	.569
New Orleans	74–61	.548
Mobile	67–69	.493
Memphis	66–73	.475
Chattanooga	65–73	.471
Birmingham	59–77	.434
Nashville	55–83	.399

1920		
Little Rock	88–59	.599
New Orleans	86–62	.581
Atlanta	85–62	.578
Birmingham	85–69	.552
Memphis	72–77	.484
Mobile	68–86	.441
Nashville	65–89	.422
Chattanooga	53–98	.351

1921		
Memphis	104–59	.679
New Orleans	97–57	.630
Birmingham	90–63	.558
Little Rock	74–77	.490
Atlanta	73–78	.483
Nashville	62–90	.409
Mobile	58–94	.382
Chattanooga	52–102	.338

1922		
Mobile	97–55	.638
Memphis	94–58	.618
New Orleans	89–64	.582
Little Rock	86–67	.562
Birmingham	74–80	.481
Chattanooga	59–93	.388
Nashville	56–96	.368
Atlanta	55–97	.362

1923		
Memphis	104–49	.680
Atlanta	99–54	.647
New Orleans	93–60	.647
Nashville	93–60	.510
Mobile	68–84	.447
Chattanooga	63–89	.414
Birmingham	54–98	.356
Little Rock	51–101	.336

1924		
New Orleans	89–57	.610
Mobile	88–66	.571
Memphis	76–70	.521
Atlanta	78–73	.516
Birmingham	75–74	.503
Nashville	75–77	.493
Chattanooga	68–83	.417
Little Rock	53–92	.365

1925		
Atlanta	87–67	.565
New Orleans	85–68	.556
Nashville	81–72	.529
Memphis	80–73	.523
Mobile	73–78	.483
Chattanooga	71–82	.464
Birmingham	67–85	.441
Little Rock	67–86	.438

1926		
New Orleans	101–53	.656
Memphis	95–57	.625
Birmingham	87–61	.588
Nashville	83–68	.550
Atlanta	76–76	.497
Chattanooga	55–94	.369
Mobile	56–96	.368
Little Rock	51–98	.342

1927		
New Orleans	96–57	.627
Birmingham	91–63	.591
Memphis	89–64	.582
Nashville	84–69	.549
Atlanta	70–81	.484
Mobile	67–87	.435
Chattanooga	59–94	.386
Little Rock	56–97	.366

1928		
Birmingham	99–54	.647
Memphis	97–55	.638
New Orleans	73–74	.497
Mobile	74–76	.493
Little Rock	72–82	.468
Chattanooga	67–85	.441
Atlanta	66–87	.431
Nashville	59–94	.386

1929		
Birmingham	93–60	.608
Nashville	90–63	.588
New Orleans	89–64	.582
Memphis	88–66	.571
Atlanta	78–75	.510
Little Rock	63–91	.409
Mobile	57–95	.375
Chattanooga	55–99	.357

1930		
Memphis	98–55	.641
New Orleans	91–61	.599
Birmingham	85–68	.556
Atlanta	84–69	.549
Little Rock	81–73	.526
Chattanooga	67–87	.435
Nashville	66–87	.431
Mobile	40–112	.263

1931		
Birmingham	97–55	.638
Little Rock	87–66	.569
Memphis	84–69	.549
Chattanooga	79–74	.516
New Orleans	78–75	.510
Atlanta	78–76	.506
Knoxville	57–94	.377
Nashville	51–102	.333

1932		
Chattanooga	98–51	.658
Memphis	101–53	.569
Little Rock	84–69	.549
Nashville	75–78	.490
Birmingham	68–83	.450
New Orleans	66–84	.440
Atlanta	62–90	.408
Knoxville	60–93	.392

1933		
Memphis	95–58	.621
New Orleans	88–65	.575
Birmingham	76–75	.533
Nashville	75–69	.521
Birmingham	76–75	.533
Chattanooga	74–77	.423
Knoxville	68–82	.453
Atlanta	62–86	.419
Little Rock	62–90	.408

1934		
New Orleans	94–60	.610
Nashville	87–65	.579
Memphis	79–72	.523
Chattanooga	78–75	.509
Atlanta	77–74	.509
Knoxville	73–80	.477
Birmingham	64–90	.416
Little Rock	59–95	.383

1935		
Atlanta	91–60	.605
New Orleans	86–67	.562
Memphis	84–70	.545
Nashville	82–69	.543
Chattanooga	75–75	.500
Little Rock	75–78	.490
Birmingham	59–95	.385
Knoxville	57–95	.375

1936		
Atlanta	94–59	.614
Nashville	86–65	.570
Birmingham	82–70	.539
New Orleans	81–71	.533
Little Rock	77–76	.503
Knoxville	63–87	.420
Chattanooga	64–89	.418
Memphis	60–90	.400

1937		
Little Rock	97–55	.595
Memphis	88–64	.579
Atlanta	84–66	.560
New Orleans	84–66	.560
Nashville	80–73	.523
Birmingham	75–76	.497
Chattanooga	56–95	.371
Knoxville	42–111	.274

1938		
Atlanta	91–62	.595
Nashville	84–66	.560
New Orleans	79–70	.530
Memphis	77–75	.507
Little Rock	75–76	.497
Birmingham	73–79	.480
Chattanooga	66–85	.437
Knoxville	59–91	.393

1939		
Chattanooga	85–65	.567
Memphis	84–67	.556
Nashville	85–68	.555
Atlanta	83–67	.553
Knoxville	79–73	.520
Little Rock	68–83	.450
Birmingham	64–89	.418
New Orleans	57–93	.380

1940		
Nashville	101–47	.682
Atlanta	93–58	.616
Memphis	79–72	.523
Chattanooga	73–79	.480
New Orleans	71–80	.470
Birmingham	70–81	.464
Little Rock	59–90	.396
Knoxville	57–96	.373

1941		
Atlanta	99–55	.643
Nashville	83–70	.542
New Orleans	78–75	.510
Chattanooga	78–76	.506
Birmingham	73–79	.480
Little Rock	71–82	.464
Memphis	69–85	.448
Knoxville	62–91	.405

1942		
Little Rock	87–59	.596
Nashville	85–66	.563
Birmingham	79–73	.520
New Orleans	77–73	.513
Atlanta	76–78	.494
Memphis	72–80	.474
Chattanooga	66–86	.434
Knoxville	61–88	.409

1943		
Nashville	83–55	.601
New Orleans	78–58	.573
Little Rock	78–62	.557
Montgomery	69–70	.496
Knoxville	65–71	.478
Birmingham	63–76	.453
Atlanta	60–79	.432
Memphis	56–81	.409

1944		
Atlanta	86–53	.619
Memphis	84–55	.609
Nashville	79–61	.564
Little Rock	66–72	.478
Birmingham	64–75	.460
Mobile	63–74	.459
Chattanooga	57–83	.409
New Orleans	57–83	.409

1945		
Atlanta	94–46	.671
Chattanooga	85–55	.607
Mobile	74–65	.532
New Orleans	73–67	.521
Memphis	68–72	.486
Birmingham	58–82	.414
Nashville	55–84	.396
Little Rock	52–88	.371

1946		
Atlanta	96–58	.623
Memphis	90–63	.588
Chattanooga	79–73	.520
New Orleans	75–77	.493
Nashville	75–78	.490
Mobile	75–78	.490
Birmingham	68–84	.447
Little Rock	52–99	.344

1947			1948			1949		
Mobile	94–59	.614	Nashville	95–58	.621	Nashville	95–57	.625
New Orleans	93–59	.612	Memphis	92–61	.601	Birmingham	91–62	.595
Nashville	80–73	.523	Birmingham	84–69	.549	Mobile	82–69	.543
Chattanooga	79–75	.513	Mobile	75–75	.500	New Orleans	77–75	.507
Atlanta	73–78	.483	New Orleans	70–83	.458	Atlanta	71–82	.464
Birmingham	73–80	.477	Atlanta	69–85	.448	Little Rock	69–85	.448
Memphis	69–85	.448	Little Rock	67–83	.447	Memphis	65–88	.425
Little Rock	51–103	.331	Chattanooga	58–96	.377	Chattanooga	60–92	.395

1950			1951			1952		
Atlanta	92–69	.609	Little Rock	93–60	.608	Chattanooga	86–66	.566
Birmingham	87–62	.584	Birmingham	83–71	.539	Atlanta	82–72	.532
Nashville	86–64	.572	Mobile	80–74	.519	Mobile	80–73	.523
Memphis	81–70	.536	Memphis	79–75	.513	Memphis	81–74	.522
New Orleans	71–79	.473	Nashville	78–76	.506	New Orleans	80–75	.516
Mobile	70–79	.470	Atlanta	76–78	.494	Nashville	73–79	.480
Chattanooga	59–89	.399	New Orleans	64–90	.418	Little Rock	68–85	.444
Little Rock	52–96	.351	Chattanooga	62–91	.405	Birmingham	64–90	.416

1953			1954			1955		
Memphis	87–67	.565	Atlanta	94–60	.610	Memphis	90–63	.588
Nashville	85–69	.552	New Orleans	92–62	.597	Birmingham	88–65	.575
Atlanta	84–70	.545	Birmingham	81–70	.536	Chattanooga	80–74	.519
Birmingham	78–76	.506	Memphis	80–74	.519	Mobile	79–75	.513
New Orleans	76–78	.494	Chattanooga	75–76	.497	Nashville	77–74	.510
Chattanooga	73–81	.474	Little Rock	64–90	.416	New Orleans	70–84	.455
Mobile	66–87	.431	Nashville	64–90	.416	Atlanta	70–84	.455
Little Rock	66–87	.431	Mobile	63–91	.409	Little Rock	51–102	.338

1956			1957			1958		
Atlanta	89–65	.578	Atlanta	87–67	.565	Birmingham	91–62	.595
Memphis	82–72	.532	Memphis	86–67	.562	Mobile	84–68	.553
Mobile	82–73	.529	Nashville	83–69	.546	Atlanta	84–70	.545
Birmingham	81–74	.523	Chattanooga	83–70	.542	Chattanooga	77–76	.503
New Orleans	79–75	.513	Mobile	75–78	.490	Nashville	76–78	.494
Chattanooga	76–78	.494	Birmingham	74–79	.484	Little Rock	74–80	.481
Nashville	75–79	.487	Little Rock	64–88	.421	Memphis	69–84	.451
Montgomery	53–101	.344	New Orleans	60–94	.390	New Orleans	57–94	.377

1959		
Birmingham	92–61	.601
Mobile	89–63	.586
Nashville	84–64	.568
Memphis	76–77	.497
Shreveport	75–79	.487
New Orleans	68–81	.456
Chattanooga	67–86	.438
Atlanta	56–96	.368

1960		
Atlanta	87–67	.565
Shreveport	86–67	.562
Little Rock	82–69	.543
Birmingham	83–70	.542
Mobile	79–72	.523
Nashville	71–82	.464
Memphis	59–87	.404
Chattanooga	60–93	.392

1961		
Chattanooga	90–62	.592
Birmingham	89–63	.586
Little Rock	80–73	.523
Atlanta	77–74	.510
Macon	75–79	.487
Nashville	69–83	.454
Shreveport	69–84	.451
Mobile	61–92	.399

1962		
Jacksonville	94–60	.610
Toronto	91–62	.595
Atlanta	83–71	.539
Rochester	82–72	.532
Columbus	80–74	.519
Buffalo	73–80	.477
Richmond	59–95	.383
Syracuse	53–101	.344

1963		
Northern Division		
Syracuse	80–70	.533
Toronto	76–75	.503
Rochester	75–76	.497
Richmond	66–81	.490
Southern Division		
Indianapolis	86–67	.562
Atlanta	85–68	.556
Arkansas	78–73	.517
Columbus	75–73	.507
Jacksonville	56–91	.381

1964		
Jacksonville	89–62	.589
Syracuse	88–66	.571
Buffalo	80–69	.537
Rochester	82–72	.532
Toronto	80–72	.526
Columbus	68–85	.444
Richmond	65–88	.425
Atlanta	55–93	.372

1965		
Columbus	85–61	.582
Atlanta	83–64	.565
Toronto	81–64	.556
Syracuse	74–73	.503
Rochester	73–74	.497
Jacksonville	71–76	.483
Toledo	68–78	.466
Buffalo	51–96	.347

Atlanta Crackers vs.
the Southern Association's All-Star Team in Atlanta

1938	1941	1946
Crackers Manager:	Crackers Manager:	Crackers Manager:
Paul Richards	Paul Richards	Hazen Cuyler
All-Star Manager:	All-Star Manager:	All-Star Manager:
"Doc" Prothro	Larry Gilbert	Bert Niehoff
Final Score Atlanta: 14–4	Final Score Atlanta: 5–0	Final Score Atlanta: 4–0
Atlanta attendance: 15,045	Atlanta attendance: 6,940	Atlanta attendance: 16,541

1950	1954	
Crackers Manager:	Crackers Manager:	
Fred Walker	Whitlow Wyatt	
All-Star Manager:	All-Star Manager:	
Pinky Higgins	Hugh Poland	
Final Score Atlanta: 8–2	Final Score Atlanta: 9–1	
Atlanta attendance: 15,295	Atlanta attendance: 16,808	

Atlanta Batting Champs in the Southern League: 1885–1899

1896	John Cline	.353	1896	Darby Knowles	.358

Atlanta Stolen Base Champs in the Southern League: 1885–1899

1886	Blondy Purcell	72

192

Atlanta Crackers Championship Teams

1907	1909	1913
William Smith, manager 78–54 (.591)	William Smith, manager 87–49 (.640)	William Smith, manager 81–56 (.691)
1917	**1919**	**1925**
Charley Frank, manager 98–56 (.636)	Charley Frank, manager 85–53 (.616)	Bert Niehoff, manager 87–67 (.565)
1935	**1936**	**1938**
Eddie Moore, manager 91–60 (.603)	Eddie Moore, manager 94–59 (.614)	Paul Richards, manager 91–62 (.595)
1941	**1945**	**1946**
Paul Richards, manager 99–55 (.643)	Hazen Cuyler, manager 94–46 (.671)	Hazen Cuyler, manager 96–58 (.623)
1950	**1954**	**1956**
Fred "Dixie" Walker, manager 92–59 (.609)	Whitlow Wyatt, manager 94–60 (610)	Clyde King, manager 89–65 (.578)
1957	**1960**	**1962**
Buddy Bates, manager 87–67 (.565)	Rube Walker, manager 87–67 (.565)	Joe Scholtz, manager 83–71 (.539)

Atlanta Crackers in the Dixie Series

1925		1935		1938	
Fort Worth	4 games	Oklahoma City	4 games	Atlanta	4 games
Atlanta	2 games	Atlanta	2 games	Beaumont, Texas	0
1946		**1954**		**1956**	
Dallas	4 games	Atlanta	4 games	Houston	4 games
Atlanta	0	Houston	3 games	Atlanta	3 games
1957					
Houston	4 games				
Atlanta	2 games				

Atlanta Crackers Leaders in Doubles

1928 Jim Poole 42	1944 Lindsey Deal 40	1951 Jack Dittmer 42

Atlanta Crackers Leaders in Most Runs Scored

1909 Dick Bayless 85	1912 King Bailey 89	1913 Tommy Long 112
1924 Ben Paschal 136	1925 Frank Zoeller 131	1939 Emil Mailho 122
1940 Emil Mailho 144	1944 Billy Goodman 122	1945 Ted Cieslak 127
1946 Lloyd Gearhart 139	1950 Gene Verble 118	

Atlanta Crackers Leaders in Stolen Bases

1907 Dode Paskert 50	1949 Ralph Brown 33	1960 Gene Wallace 14

Atlanta Crackers Leaders in Triples

1913 Billy Smith 16	1915 Roy Moran 20	1931 Doug Taitt 19
1939 Russ Peters 15	1944 Billy Goodman, Mel Ivy 13	1946 Lloyd Gearhart 17

Atlanta Cracker Pitchers Who Led the League in Lowest ERAs

1935 Harry Kelley 2.50	1936 Luther Thomas 2.82	1938 Tom Sunkel 2.33
1941 Emile Lochbaum 2.74	1945 Lew Carpenter 1.82	1953 Art Fowler 3.03
1961 Jack Smith 2.09		

Atlanta Cracker Pitchers Who Led the League in Most Victories

1940 Frank Smith	31	**1916** Scott Perry	24	**1920** Tom Sheehan	26
1924 Ray Francis	24	**1929** Climax Blethen	22	**1934** Harry Kelley	23
1938 Tom Sunkel	21	**1941** Ed Huesser	20	**1945** Lew Carpenter	22
1946 Mickey McGowen	22	**1948** Norman Brown	22	**1954** Leo Crisante	24
1958 Bob Hartman	20	**1960** Pete Richert	19		

Atlanta Crackers Pitchers Who Led the League in Strikeouts

1925 George Pipgras	141	**1938** Tom Sunkel	178	**1960** Pete Richert	251

Atlanta Cracker Pitchers Who Led the League in Winning Percentage

1904	1906	1907
Frank Smith 31-10, .786	Tom Hughes 25-5, .833	Roy Castleton 17-8, .680
1909	**1919**	**1936**
Oliver Jones 20-7, .740	Tom Sheehan 17-3, .850	Dutch Leonard 13-3, .813
1938	**1945**	**1954**
Tom Sunkel 21-5, .808	Lew Carpenter 22-2, .917	Leo Crisante 24-7, .774

Atlanta Crackers RBI Leaders in the Southern Association

1929 Jim Poole	127	**1941** Les Burge	146	**1944** Lindsey Deal	124
1945 Ted Cieslak	120	**1953** William Sinovic	126		

Atlanta Crackers Hitting Champions in the Southern Association

1912 Harry Welchonce	157	**1913** Harry Welchonce	194	**1925** Wilbur Goode	236
1927 Roy Moran	177	**1937** Hugh Luby	208	**1944** Lindsey Deal	190
1950 Ben Thorpe	195	**1953** William Sinovic	201		

SELECT BIBLIOGRAPHY

Research Facilities

The Atlanta Historical Society

The Chico Renfroe Collection at Auburn Avenue Research Library, Atlanta

Books

Allen, Frederick. *Atlanta Rising: The Invention of an International City: 1946–1996*. Atlanta: Longstreet Press, 1996.

Bisher, Furman. *Miracle in Atlanta: The Atlanta Braves Story*. Cleveland: World Publishing Co., 1966.

Garrett, Franklin M. *Atlanta and Environs: A Chronicle of Its People and Events*. 2 vols. New York: Lewis Historical Publishing Co., 1954.

Holway, John. *Voices from the Great Black Baseball Leagues*. New York: Da Capo, 1992.

Johnson, Harry. *Standing the Gaff: The Life and Hard Times of a Minor League Umpire*. Lincoln: University of Nebraska Press, 1994.

Kuhn, Clifford M., Harlon E. Joyce, and E. Bernard West. *Living Atlanta: An Oral History of the City, 1914–1948*. Atlanta: Atlanta Historical Society and Athens: University of Georgia Press, 1990.

The Official International League Record Book.

The Official Southern League Record Book.

O'Neal, Bill. *The Southern League: Baseball in Dixie, 1885–1994*. Burnet, Texas: Eakin Press, 1992.

Peterson, Robert. *The Negro Leagues Book*.

Reidenbaugh, Lowell. *Take Me Out to the Ball Park*. St. Louis, Mo.: Sporting News Publishing Co., 1983.

Reiss, Steven A. *Touching Base: Professional Baseball and American Culture in the Progressive Era*. Westport, Conn.: Greenwood, 1980.

Rogosin, Donn. *Invisible Men: Life in Baseball's Negro Leagues*. New York: Atheneum, 1983.

Rosenberg, David Michael. *Crumbs and Crackers: A Study of Baseball in Atlanta*.

Roth, Darlene R., and Ambrose, Andy. *Metropolitan Frontiers: A Short History of Atlanta*. Atlanta: Longstreet Press, 1996.

Sullivan, Dean A., comp. and ed. *Middle Innings: A Documentary History of Baseball, 1900–1948*. Lincoln: University of Nebraska Press, 1998.

Thorn, John. *The Complete Armchair Book of Baseball*. New York: Galahad Books, 1997.

Ward, Geoffrey C. and Ken Burns. *Baseball: An Illustrated History*. New York: Knopf, 1994.

Wright, Wade H. *History of the Georgia Power Company: 1855–1956*. Atlanta: Georgia Power Company, 1957.

Periodicals

Atlanta Constitution
Atlanta Daily World
Atlanta Historical Bulletin
Atlanta Journal
Atlanta Journal Magazine
City Builder
New York Times

Research Papers

Steve Beaupre. *The 1938 Black Crackers: Atlanta Baseball's Unknown Champion*. Unpublished thesis.

ACKNOWLEDGMENTS

Special thanks to Patrick Allen, Thomas Payton, and the professionals of Hill Street Press for their faith in this project. They have the highest standards of quality and excellence, and I hope this book lives up to their expectations.

Stephen Schmidt, "Mr. Oglethorpe University," for the use of his *Official Southern Association Record Book* for my research.

The family and friends of "Mr. Atlanta Baseball," the late Earl Mann, a pioneer in the most honorable sense of the word, and one of the few men of whom I've never heard a discouraging word.

Cyrus Daniels, Jonathan Phillips and my friends at VISIONS USA, for their valuable information on another unheralded, courageous group of trailblazers, the Atlanta Black Crackers.

The countless players, fans and journalists who were gracious enough to share their memories with me.

And my family and many longtime friends for their support when it comes to my good—and not-so-good—ideas.